Discovering the Water of Life

BRENT MASSEY

Published by Jetlag Press

Massey, Brent.
     Discovering the Water of Life / Brent Massey.
     p. cm.
     Includes index
     1. Christianity 2. Christian Dream interpretation 3. Victory in Christ 4. Holy Spirit 5. Typology (Pychology). 6. Myers-Briggs Type Indicator. 7. Culture types 8. International Culture. I. Title.
     ISBN 0-9790397-3-8

Printed in the USA and UK

http://www.brentmassey.com

DEDICATION

This is dedicated to the Lord and my family.

ALSO BY BRENT MASSEY

Culture Shock! Hawai'i

Where in the World Do I Belong??

Contents

Faith Runs in the Family

Since I wrote a book on Christianity, I wanted to see how faith ran in my family. My mother is a historian and researched our family's genealogy. I have at least three ministers in my family.

My great-great-grandfather, Robert Calvin Mount, was a Methodist minister. In 1872, he helped plant the first Methodist church in Chico Texas. In 1899, my great-grandparents, Mary Alice Mount (daughter of Robert Calvin Mount) and Claude Oliver Huff married in Chico, Texas. At age 37, after serving in the war and farming until 1912, Claude became an ordained Methodist minister through a correspondence course. He preached in Oklahoma and Texas and died in 1945.

This is a photo of my great-grandfather, John Jackson Russell, and great grandmother, Susannah Robins Russell. Susannah was 3/4 Cherokee Indian (in the picture that is a feather in her hair). John was a circuit riding Baptist minister in the Ozark hills of Arkansas and a civil war veteran (see the medals on his lapel). John got measles during the civil war and became blind. My great-grandmother would read the Bible to him to prepare for his sermons, and as a youth, my grandfather led his father's horse from village to village to preach.

Water of Life

D.L. Moody said the best class of Christian has not only accepted and surrendered but also has the water of life flowing from them.

To all who are thirsty I will give freely from the springs of the water of life. All who are victorious will inherit all these blessings, and I will be their God, and they will be my children. (Revelations 21:6-7)

Before I received the baptism of the Holy Spirit, I was moved by sunny days, the beauty of the ocean, and the wonder of my children—all God's creations. Now that I am walking in the Holy Spirit, those things still move me but pale in comparison to knowing God through the power and the fruit of the Holy Spirit.

This is only scratches the surface of how much more satisfying the water of life is than anything the world has to offer. From the viewpoint of personality type, as a feeling type I used emotional release and romantic love as a way to temporarily relieve or fill up the emptiness that only the water of life (the Holy Spirit) could fill permanently.

I relieved myself through dumping emotions with a therapist, but that was temporary relief because only God can provide permanent healing and transformation through His indwelling Holy Spirit. Contrary to what psychology teaches us, healing doesn't come from emotional release it comes from the Holy Spirit.

Different personality types try to fill the emptiness in different ways.

I also tried to fill the void with feelings or emotions of romantic love. Emotions, like thoughts, are natural and part of our soul—even God experiences anger and other emotions, for example: You must worship no other gods, for the Lord, whose very name is Jealous, is a God who is jealous about his relationship with you (Exodus 34:14). Even though emotions are natural they can't fill the emptiness in our spirit—only He can.

Different personality types try to fill the emptiness in different ways: thinking types might use success and status, and sensing types probably use excitement and material possessions. As a feeling type, I used sex and food for comfort—whereas, for a sensing type, that might be a sensual pleasure, but both are still temporary and increasingly not satisfying.

Don't be drunk with wine, because that will ruin your life. Instead, be filled with the Holy Spirit. (Ephesians 5:18)

Intuitive types, like myself, escape through intellectual pursuits, fantasy, and imagination. My passion for writing and the search for intellectual understanding and universal truth becomes progressively less fulfilling if I try to use it to fill the emptiness. These are only a few examples of the way we stop the water of life (the Holy Spirit) from flowing in and through us by trying to fill ourselves with temporary worldly things.

This can also be seen on a culture types level too. The sensing Japanese use food, sex, and consumerism as a way to temporarily fill the emptiness. When something loses its sensing appeal there is always a new product (food, technology, etc.), new fashion trend, or new celebrity being rolled out. A culture, like a person, can go to extremes looking for that original high. The extremes in Japanese pornography is an example of how far this culture has gone seeking to fill the emptiness. The Japanese also idolize consumerism—just look at the tourists in Hawaii with armfuls of shopping bags.

The thinking American culture type, instead of turning to the Holy Spirit for lasting satisfaction, creates the static of ongoing diversions in their life like the Japanese, but in a more thinking way, for example, through increasing work commitments and trying to pay for larger houses and cars. Americans also desensitize themselves to the voice of the Holy Spirit through escalating graphic violence in the media (movies, news, images of war, etc.).

Ask and we shall receive. Ask God for His living water and we will be filled with it and the emptiness and related feelings will go away. The water of life is answer for all personality types and culture types.

Then the angel showed me a river with the water of life, clear as crystal, flowing from the throne of God and of the Lamb. It flowed down the center of the main street. On each side of the river grew a tree of life, bearing twelve crops of fruit, with a fresh crop each month. The leaves were used for medicine to heal the nations. (Revelation 22:1-2).

The angel showed me a river with the water of life.

1

Christianity and Myers-Briggs personality types

I flipped through last month's issue of the magazine Psychology Today; there were articles and editorials on a myriad of psychological problems yet none of the psychological explanations and answers contain any spiritual solutions (or mention of Christianity or even God). At the last Association of Psychological Type (APT) conference only 6% of the participants reported a primary interest area of Religion and Spirituality (as opposed to 41% interest in Management and Organizational Development). Several members of the Honolulu MBTI group are agnostic or atheist.

The MBTI was originally based on Carl Jung's theories. My MBTI qualifying course instructor told us, "Jung is not God; he is a man with a theory." She also said type is the energy under the behavior. Anyone can do the behavior, but your type determines whether you use more or less energy to do the behavior. I take this one step farther by saying the spirit is the energy under the type. People talk about functions, mental processes and personality type as being your true source and flow of energy. That is deceiving because the real source of energy for the soul comes from our spirit and whatever your spirit is grounded in. If your centered on self, your spirit will be powered by self-will power, but if it is centered on God, your spirit will be filled with God's spirit and the infinite power and will of God.

David Tacey wrote in his book, *How to Read Jung* (2006), that Jung believed in God and his father was a Christian minister. However, Jung believed that Christianity wasn't the only "sacred force".

The real source of energy for the soul comes from our spirit.

He also believed the virgin birth and resurrection are metaphors or symbols instead of actual historical fact. Based on the miracles I have experienced in my own life, I believe in the infinite power of God and the miracles written in the Bible. Tacey sees religion as the blazing light of the sun and without it we are just using the stars for direction: that is to say our dreams, intuition, and looking for signs in everyday life. I was saved, or came to accept Christ, as a teenager but hadn't surrendered to God. I spent many years on a self-powered search for my calling, relying heavily on intuition, signs, dreams and the insights of others. I called upon God for guidance and help frequently but it was a long journey guided only by distant twinkles of light. According to Tacey, Jung believed, "A relationship with the sacred provides meaning and direction to the soul." Jung seems to suggest a mix of self and a "relationship" with God instead of accepting the power of God as the sole source of spiritual power. This is where Jung missed the boat: a relationship with "sacred forces" is still an individual being guided only by starlight.

When I read the book *The Handbook to Happiness* (1971) by Dr. Charles Solomon, it was like a hot, molten, shimmering sun breaking over the horizon in my weary, tear-filled eyes. Solomon explained that carnal Christians have accepted Christ, yet not completely surrendered to Christ. The problem with Jung's theory is that the self is still at the center of our life even when we have a "relationship" with God. According to Solomon, "the soul, in and of itself, is neutral. Whatever is placed at the center, Something or Christ, becomes the driving force that empowers the soul, determining its attitudes and actions and the ultimate worth of that which results." That "Something" can be self or other people we think make us happy (spouse, children, boyfriend, girlfriend, etc.) or success, work, sex, drugs, etc. "Self in the center of the life means we are in control or, at least, are trying to be."

Solomon explains man as a tri-unity of body, soul and spirit. What's confusing about Jung is that he mixes soul and spirit. Also, his archetypes seem to lie somewhere on the border between soul and spirit. According to Solomon the body is physiological (world-conscious), the soul is psychological (self-conscious), and the spirit is spiritual (God-conscious). The spirit is what empowers the soul and the soul is what empowers the body. The soul is the container for mind, emotions, and will; and the center of our psychology, abnormal psychology, and personality type (Jung, Myers-Briggs, etc.). Many psychologists, and personality type professionals fail to recognize the most important and most powerful part of the tri-unity of man: The Spirit! It powers the soul and everything else. Solomon rightly states that through surrender to Christ an individual's abnormal psychology and behaviors dissipate. Tacey reports that Jung also believed in the "spiritual dimension of healing." "Jung believed that meaning and 'spirit' can heal psychic illness and even bring relief to physical disease." Solomon explains in detail the problem with modern day psychology and counseling: an attempt to fix self and various psychological and physiological symptoms instead of addressing the underlying spiritual emptiness.

> "Look for yourself, and you will find in the long run only hatred, loneliness, despair, rage, ruin, and decay. But look for Christ and you will find Him, and with Him everything else thrown in" –C.S. Lewis (Mere Christianity 1952).

I poured over self-help books (on addiction, happiness, self actualization, etc.) for answers to the emptiness inside that manifested itself in my work and relationships. I spent seven years in counseling believing that psychology must have the answers, but I never felt any relief. I believed that if I found work I was passionate about, it would stop the inner voices, negative thoughts, confusing emotions and desires to escape (through porn, sex, food, or whatever). I read Po Bronson's bestselling self-help book, What Should I Do With My Life? (2003); it explored the various ways people find their calling and what they decide to dedicate their life to. Bronson has a wonderful book filled with insight and personal stories but is missing the spiritual component just like the Psychology Today magazine, the MBTI type community, and even the small Honolulu MBTI group. I believe the emptiness (of many of the people profiled in Bronson's book) is not in their vocation but is a calling towards God; and for those that already know God it's a calling towards complete surrender and complete faith.

> *The emptiness is not in your vocation but is a calling towards God.*

Jung believed a relationship with God shouldn't be controlled by or depend on religious institutions. However, trying to have a relationship with God outside the body of the church is, according to Pastor Mike Kai of Hope Chapel West Oahu, like taking a lung out of the body: the body survives (although struggles) and the lung soon withers away and dies. Spiritual victory is through complete surrender to Christ. Going to church and reading the Bible keeps you on the path of victory. I avoided Christians because the majority didn't seem to be living victorious lives. I had long rejected religion, yet not God, because I felt the church was a house of hypocrites. I failed, because "Anyone who denies the Son doesn't have the Father" (1 John 2:23 NLT)—you can't have God without accepting Christ and thus Christianity.

One black preacher, from Cote Devoir (Africa), explained that the church was not a house of saints but more like a hospital for the sick. Christians who are saved but not surrendered are the same as sinners who are not in the church: they are operating their lives from their own self willpower instead of surrendering to complete faith in God, allowing Him to work in and through them to achieve his will in their lives. (This of course is a big step and is made much easier when we are at the end of our rope and completely given up on trying to make things work on our own.) "It is estimated that 90 percent of all Christians never experience the abundant or victorious life, so they do not understand how deep psychological problems can be resolved by letting the Lord Jesus Christ manifest his life in them, rather than resorting to human therapy" (*The Handbook to Happiness*).

In my years of searching I wandered across diverse career paths and even studied personality type looking for an answer to the calling in my soul. Yet, I didn't realize that the human spirit powers the soul. Whatever you fill your spirit with will create outcomes in the way you express your soul to the world. My spirit was empty. I frequently prayed to God asking for his help and his will for my life but I rejected the Bible, the church, and Christians. Eventually, my marriage and finances came to a crisis. I had tried everything possible and there was nothing left I could do, then my mother gave me the gift of the book *Handbook to Happiness: A Biblical Guide to Victorious Living*. I frowned at the overt Christian nature of it, but one night I couldn't sleep because of the emotional pain in my life so I picked up Solomon's book and began read it all night. The tears streamed down my face as I saw myself in the book, my misconception of psychology having the answers, my struggle with self control of my addictive behaviors, worries, fears, obsessive thoughts but most of all my complete misunderstanding of Christianity.

I had accepted Christ when I was 13 but I didn't find spiritual victory in Christ until 25 years later. Why? I hadn't been to church in 23 years. During high school, I spent a couple years in A.A. trying to accept to the will of God using the twelve steps program. A.A. taught me how to self-define my own religion and that led to and justified my rejection of Christianity. Once again, you can't have God without accepting Christ. Twelve step programs are half-truths that deceive us and keep us away from the truth of Christ.

> *A.A. taught me how to self-define my own religion.*

Psychology is the same, it can be used to understand people but only spiritual-therapy through victory in Christ has true healing and the answer to all our problems. I had believed in God but only saw Him as an external force to be negotiated with and prayed to. I never understood the concept of complete surrender of control of my life to Him, allowing Him to work through me instead of trying to do what I thought he wanted me to do. The center of my life had been on self, and later my marriage and my wife—all of these being imperfect and inevitably failing me—then I put God in the center of my life and filled my spirit with the Holy Spirit through surrender to Jesus Christ. Addictions, obsessive relationships, fears, anxiety, anger, suspicion, were all overcome through Christ. The inner voices were calmed, and the desperate searching alternating with various escapes (work, porn, sex, food, etc.) ended. Psychological and physiological problems are healed through complete surrender to and faith in Christ.

Without a spiritual foundation centered on God we are more often acting or working through the dark-side of our personality type and archetypes. I suggest that before you apply personality type theories in your life, you first understand your spiritual power source. If you base your spiritual power on anything other than complete surrender to and faith in God, your struggles with personal problems, marital problems, occupational problems, and other relationships will not improve because you are only treating the psychological or physiological symptoms instead of the underlying spiritual emptiness. I urge you to read Dr. Solomon's book, *The Handbook to Happiness*, especially if you are interested in psychology, counseling or even Christian counseling. Solomon explains how all these therapies are ineffective because they strengthen a reliance on self instead of on God: a life centered on God, surrendered to Christ, and complete faith in the infinitely powerful grace of God. Basically, we dedicate our spirit to Christ and our sins are forgiven, and when we surrender our life to Christ our mind is renewed. It is through this renewal of the mind that mental and physical healing occurs. Jung believed that a relationship with God made this mental and physical healing possible, but he missed the point that only total surrender to and complete faith in God makes that possible.

Charles Trumbull discovered this truth in 1910 and wrote it in his book *Victory in Christ* (1959): "It meant I need never again ask Him to help me as though He were apart from me. Instead I could ask Him simply to do His work and His will in me and with me and through me. My body was His, my mind His, my will His, my spirit His. And not merely His, but literally a part of Him." I highly recommend this little 90-page book as a great introduction to this spiritual life change and especially to Christians who still feel something is missing in their walk with Christ.

Christianity and personality type

I asked many questions and went to more extremes in thoughts and ideas before I surrendered and went back to church. It was as if I was projecting the inner need I had for God into judging others through extreme ideals. I had made my ideals my rock but now God is my rock.

I am a MBTI Qualified Practitioner, and after surrendering to the Lord, I wondered if I should forget everything I learned about the MBTI because personality type theory originated from a non-Christian (Carl Jung).

God can use anything for His glory.

Despite the fact that psychology is a godless discipline and Jung wasn't Christian, that doesn't mean God can't use it for His glory. He can use anything He wants—human wisdom, half-truths, lies, and anything else the enemy might spin off. He is sovereign and all-powerful over everything. Even products of the occult can be transformed by the Lord for His purposes and glory. One author said the difference between truth and error is not a gap but a razors edge. God can extract the truth for His work and use it to His glory. He did this through the Christian woman Isabel Myers when she constructed her Myers-Briggs test.

Myers title, *Gifts Differing*, for her book on personality types, was taken from the Bible. "Having then gifts differing according to the grace that is given to us..." (Romans 12:6). This passage is about spiritual gifts. In addition to personality type indicators, many churches have tests for spiritual gifts. Those gifts and personality types may look worldly until God transforms you and He begins to show you their true meaning and application for the glory of His kingdom. Therefore, my years of studying personality type are not wasted because God will use my human knowledge for His glory.

Jung also studied dream interpretation and recorded many dream symbol definitions. God uses our dreams to speak to us. When we interpret dreams we may even use some of the theories and symbol definitions that Jung discovered, but that doesn't make our interpretation something from the enemy. Lastly, we can determine our personality type and spiritual gifts, but that doesn't mean God can't call us in a completely different direction. God may call us in a direction the very opposite of our personality type or spiritual gifts.

Masculine Christianity and Myers-Briggs thinking types.

Masculine and feminine values are a popular tool to define cultures. In my research (for my book on culture types) I found that the definition of masculine and feminine values are very narrow and limited—not to mention the confusion with feminism. Also, it's hard to get around or forget the many stereotypes of masculine and feminine values, e.g. macho. I have proven in my book, *Where in the World Do I Belong??*, that the thinking and feeling facets of personality type (Myers-Briggs MBTI) are much more detailed, descriptive, and accurate tools for describing a culture, and correlate somewhat with masculine and feminine values. These same tools can be used for describing the culture of the Christian church.

I believe men's desire for masculine Christianity is really a thinking vs. feeling conflict as opposed to a struggle between masculine and feminine values. According to the *MBTI Manual*, national statistics report 76% of women are feeling types and 57% men are thinking types. Christianity is based on feeling type preferences, such as love, kindness, understanding, humility, harmony, compassion and empathy.

Feeling is subjective mental process (not to be confused with feelings) where we make decisions based on inner values, societal values, and in our case it's Christian values.

One Christian thinking type man doesn't attend men's gatherings at the church because he doesn't like to be emotional. His wife, a balanced thinking and feeling type, acknowledges that a relationship with God is a feeling experience because it is through the heart and spirit. Isn't the path to the spirit through the heart, and our subjective nature? Thinking types have to overcome their rational objections to Christianity before they allow their heart to tell them to trust in God and the church. Once they have overcome that initial thinking objection it will still simmer in the background, but God's truth is strong enough in their heart that those objections can now be ignored. This is how a thinking type—whether man or woman—comes to accept and surrender to Christ. For a feeling type, it is a direct route to the heart, we feel the Holy Spirit in the praise and worship, and the compassion of the Christian fellowship. We may still question the Bible but our critical, objective side doesn't have to be overcome before we can believe Christ is our life.

I demonstrated in my book, *Where in the World Do I Belong??*, that America is a thinking culture type; people in our culture expect thinking behavior and styles of communication. The Christian church, on the other hand, is a feeling culture type: personal, gentle, harmonious, tolerant, compassionate, empathetic, etc. As a feeling man I have been a discriminated against in a thinking-man, American culture; conversely, thinking men feel discriminated against in the feeling Christian culture. I feel for you guys (no pun intended), but it's not a matter of changing the Christian culture or the church, it's a matter of developing cross-cultural skills. And yes, everytime you are in Church you will feel like a foreigner trying to speak another language, but that pain doesn't justify attempts to change the Christian culture of the church. Every church, every corporation, and every country has it's own culture—some good and some bad. If a particular church doesn't value all gifts and discriminates against thinking types, your experiencing the same situation feeling types have in American culture. Is it possible that the feeling church compensates for the thinking extremes in American culture? If you want to bring about balance, you'll have to also change American culture.

Christianity is based on feeling type preferences.

Or is it such that worldly ways will always be represented in a thinking fashion and spiritual ones always in a feeling way—is that maybe what the Almighty had intended?

The books, *Wild at Heart* by John Eldredge, and *No More Christian Nice Guy* by Paul Coughlin, rail against feminist control of the church and Christianity (in the US). Eldredge's *Wild at Heart* has men as risk-takers and adventure-seekers, which is a narrow, masculine stereotype. Risk-taking and adventure-seeking are facets of extraverted sensing and extraverted intuitive types, which can be with either men or women. Coughlin claims that Jesus was confrontational and assertive, and I agree at times he was, but look at the Bible as a whole and the values taught are mainly along the lines of feeling type preferences: personal, gentle, merciful, harmonious, accepting, compassionate, empathetic, etc. You can pick and choose out of the Bible what you think supports your argument for a thinking or masculine church, but you would only be deceiving yourself to the overriding truths repeated throughout the Bible. Let's face it, it's God's job to have the power, to be tough and to judge us (facets of thinking and judging), and it's our job to be understanding and tender-hearted to one another, and give our praise and loyalty to God—all facets of feeling types.

If their are Christian feminists that are trying to make men passive (which I haven't seen but Coughlin and Eldredge claim there are) in the church, that is their business, between themselves and God. Love the person and hate the sin—C.S. Lewis said this is easy to do because we do it everyday with ourselves. If feminists are a thorn in the side of the thinking men, God uses that for His glory to keep those men more fully surrendered for His use. Pray to bless the lives of those that offend you, and God will show you, in you, what He wants you to see. God doesn't need us to confront others or do anything for Him. He doesn't need our help! He needs men who are fully surrender to his control so that He can effectively use them to His glory. Keep our eyes on God only! He will take care of everything else! If I discern something wrong in someone else, I pray about it. It's their business between them and God. It's not my business to confront them unless I am willing to pray about it and offer my full support and unconditional love to help them overcome their difficulty. If it's something that causes me a burden, my business is to pray

> *A Christian Nice Guy (CNG) is someone who hasn't taken his life to the cross.*

God removes this burden—if it is God's will—or control and guide me in what He wants me to do with it.

Coughlin describes his Christian Nice Guys (CNG) as passive, non-confrontational, unemotional, and unable to cry. He tells how he went through counseling to overcome his nice guy behaviors. God heals dysfunction and inferiority complexes not counselors or psychologists (even if they are Christian ones). These CNGs are just men who need to die to their old inferior self and experience the healing, transformation of the Holy Spirit. A nice guy is one who hasn't taken his life to the cross, and died to his old self and all the mental problems that were part of it. A nice guy doesn't find a "rich and satisfying life" by trying to be an assertive Christian Good Guy (CGG); he finds it through victory in Christ.

We don't need to delve so deep into the root of all the rejection in our lives. The Holy Spirit does the searching for us and according to His planning and timing will bring those issues to the surface (or consciousness). He will reveal the roots of those issues to us. Then you will see the Christian man God has really intended you to be; and anything in the church you perceive as feminism will no longer bother you. The truth of your walk will convict anyone who tries to make you anything other than what God wants you to be. Don't self-define what it is to be a Christian man, let God show you and others through your Christian walk.

Masculine Christianity is new twist on the same old carnal Christian. An assertive, strong will isn't surrender to Christ—it's through our brokenness and surrender that His Spirit is strong in us. Strength and power come from the Holy Spirit working through us, not from asserting our will or masculinity. The Bible says women are weaker and ate the forbidden apple first, but on the other hand woman are also the first to go to church. Men are a little harder to get into the church. Thinking men are naturally strong-willed, challenging, tough, firm-minded, impersonal, and critical. They are at a disadvantage in church because they have to use their inferior, immature feeling mental process. This is according to God's plan, he wants strong-willed thinking men to have this thorn in their side so that he can more effectively use them for His glory, just like He did with Paul. It is in our weakness that His spirit is strong. He uses thinking men by making them use their weaker feeling preferences, and in their weakness He can be strong.

God doesn't want to change your personality type by sending you to church. He made your personality. He wired your brain that way for a reason and His purpose. He doesn't intend to change it, but He wants to transform your character into the person He intended for you to be through a process called sanctification, which means He frees you from the power of sin, purifies you, and spiritually grows you to depend solely on His divine grace.

Why did God equip some people with a fluency in the language of Christianity and others not? Why does He give different spiritual gifts to different people? Why does God give some gifts that are rewarded in the fleshly world and other gifts that are suited for the spiritual world? It's not our place to question God or his plan—just understand His wisdom and purpose are beyond our comprehension. We are mere children and our Heavenly Father knows what is best for us.

For American thinking type men, it's kind of hard being the minority when you've spent your whole life being in the majority. It sort of blocks you from seeing there could be other ways of living and communicating—American's in particular are guilty of this. I suggest Christian men take the opportunity not to develop their feminine side but instead to develop their feeling mental process, and then you won't feel like your being told to be a feminist wimp. I'm a feeling type man and I don't feel in the least bit less masculine inside the church, but I also don't subscribe to societies definition of masculine and feminine because they are narrow and just don't fit most people. My suggestion for thinking males is to learn the language of feeling (just like you have to learn the love language of your wife) and master it. There are people in the church that speak feeling as their native language and will always feel at home, whereas you might always feel like a foreigner. Yet, take heart, because Peter (2:11) reminds us that as Christians we are all foreigners living in a foreign land.

So how do you apply Christianity in your everyday life outside of the church? Use the very cross-cultural skills you developed while at church! As a thinking man you have learned to speak the feeling language of humility, harmony, compassion and empathy at church and now you can apply it your Christian walk at work and home!

God, marriage, personality type and culture differences.

Marriage on the Rock is a great Christian marriage series that I highly recommend. Before we started going to church, I tried many things to get my marriage on track. I went to counseling to figure out and resolve my psychological issues that were getting in the way and causing problems, and I studied Japanese culture and language to better understand our cross-cultural differences. My first book *Culture Shock! Hawaii* evolved out of this search to understand cultural differences. At the same time I studied personality type as a means to better understand our differences as a couple. My second book, *Where in the World Do I Belong??*, evolved out of this search to understand personality type and cultural differences. Lastly, a marriage counselor recommended the *The Five Love Languages* book to me, and I learned all I could about the love languages.

I have a natural passion and interest in counseling, therapy and people differences such as cultural, personality type, and love languages. I used these tools to try to get my marriage on the right track, but none of it worked because I got it all backwards—we must have Jesus in our marriage first.

> *We must have Jesus in our marriage first.*

God is a trinity or triune being consisting of God, the son of God (Jesus Christ), and the Holy Spirit. God created man to be a triune being. Man is composed of a body, a soul, and a spirit. Jimmy Evans, in his *Marriage on the Rock* series, explains that God also created marriage as a triune being. Men fulfill the role of Jesus Christ (e.g. the church is the bride of Christ); and women fulfill the role of the Holy Spirit. God made woman the helper to man and Jesus called the Holy Spirit a helper (Jesus said He would send a helper in the form of the Holy Spirit). The third part of the triune is God at the center of a marriage (one that has been dedicated to Him).

Jimmy Evans states that God made man in the image of God but marriage is really the closest image of God. "Only God can meet the deepest needs in a marriage...and release the potential of your marriage." We must have God in our marriage first, then we will reap the fruit of the Holy Spirit. After that, we will see results in Christian marriage counseling and in our efforts to understand differences (cultural, personality type, and love languages).

2

Steps to Victory in Christ

Many defeated Christians don't have anyone to disciple them and may never hear the message of the cross. "They have been born again, but their behavior has not changed. Their spirit is perfect, but their soul is still messed up" (FW Handout). When we receive Christ into our life (our spirit) we are re-born spiritually; however, we don't experience victory in Christ until we make Christ the center of our lives; completely and unconditionally surrender our lives to His will; and believe that we die everyday to live in Christ and have Christ live His life in us. Many Christians become ready for the message of the cross when they reach a bottom or recognize doing it all on our own hasn't worked.

I've written and compiled the following as a study guide that is based on the concepts of Dr. Solomon's *The Handbook to Happiness*.

Steps to Victory guide
(Chapter 1 *The Handbook to Happiness*)

Romans 7:19 is the description of DEFEAT: "I want to do what is right, but I can't. I want to do what is good, but I don't. I don't want to do what is wrong, but I do it anyway." We try not to sin but we keep coming back to it.

The trouble is with me, for I am all too human, a slave to sin. I don't really understand myself, for I want to do what is right, but I don't do it. Instead, I do what I hate. But if I know that what I am doing is wrong, this shows that I agree that the law is

> *I want to do what is right, but I don't do it. Instead, I do what I hate.*

good. So I am not the one doing wrong; it is sin living in me that does it. And I know that nothing good lives in me, that is, in my sinful nature. I want to do what is right, but I can't. I want to do what is good, but I don't. I don't want to do what is wrong, but I do it anyway. But if I do what I don't want to do, I am not really the one doing wrong; it is sin living in me that does it. I have discovered this principle of life—that when I want to do what is right, I inevitably do what is wrong. I love God's law with all my heart. But there is another power within me that is at war with my mind. This power makes me a slave to the sin that is still within me. Oh, what a miserable person I am! Who will free me from this life that is dominated by sin and death? (Romans 7:14-24).

Those who live only to satisfy their own sinful nature will harvest decay and death from that sinful nature. But those who live to please the Spirit will harvest everlasting life from the Spirit (Gal. 6:8). "Indwelling sin wants to constantly convince us to listen to our emotions" (FW Handout).

According to Solomon in his book, *Handbook to Happiness*, these are some of the expressions of sin that come out of defeat: unresolved inner conflicts, inferiority and superiority complexes, depression, and anxiety. Solomon states all of these emotional results stem from REJECTION—either overtly or covertly—while growing up. Solomon in his book, *The Ins and Outs of Rejection*, describes the ways we are rejected in our families when growing up and explains the way out through experiencing the cross.

INFERIORITY complex is feelings of insecurity, insufficient, inhibited, worry, fear, and guilt. "Man believes he is inferior, unable, unsure, etc. and behaves accordingly. He is self-conscious, withdrawn, worried, fearful, unsure, etc. Often too these people are depressed" (FW Handout). There are also people who can alternate between superiority and inferiority based on their feelings.

SUPERIORITY complex is acting self-confident, perfectionistic, compulsively active, hostile, infallible, having a need for control, and having underlying anger. Ninety percent of superiority complexes are attempts to hide inferiority complexes. "Secretly this person too thinks he is inferior but he has figured out that he is better off when he is superior, better than others, at least outwardly. Often this is the case because his parents were super perfectionistic. It is common for these people to be very fearful" (FW Handout).

Complete, total, unconditional SURRENDER to Christ. (Chapter 2 *The Handbook to Happiness*)

So here's what I want you to do, God helping you: Take your everyday, ordinary life—your sleeping, eating, going-to-work, and walking-around life—and place it before God as an offering (Romans 12:1-2 MSG).

> *Place your life on the altar before God.*

Completely SURRENDER your life to God and to His will for your life. Place your life on the altar before Him to do whatever He wants. "Readily recognize what he wants from you, and quickly respond to it." Completely trust His will and plan for our lives, especially since it is better than anything we could ever figure out on our own. His ways of achieving this plan are sometimes higher and more complex than anything we could every imagine or understand. Pray a specific prayer to totally surrender your life to Him and allow God to use your life for His glory in any way He chooses.

Put Christ at the CENTER of your life and nothing else:

Don't become so well-adjusted to your culture that you fit into it without even thinking. Instead, fix your attention on God (Romans 12:1-2 MSG).

1. "Let Him live His life in you." Let Jesus "live his life in ours" (*Handbook to Happiness*). He is not 'with' me but instead I am in Him and He is in me.

2. Remove your center on self (success, significant others, addictions, things (house, car), etc.) and replace it with Christ. Push your ego to the side and center your life on the Lord. Just like the potter centers the clay on the wheel, we must move the center of our life to Christ before He can transform us into the image of Christ.

3. "Whatever is placed in the center becomes the driving force that empowers the soul, determining it's attitudes and actions and the ultimate worth of that which results" (*Handbook to Happiness*). Circumstances in life bounce off your center and produce your reactions to life. If Christ is at the center, your actions and responses (instead of reactions) are going to be Christ-like because of Christ's life in you and He is living His life through you. Christ is living in us, working through us.

Victory over sin through giving CONTROL to the Holy Spirit:

Those who are dominated by the sinful nature think about sinful things, but those who are controlled by the Holy Spirit think about things that please the Spirit. So letting your sinful nature control your mind leads to death. But letting the Spirit control your mind leads to life and peace (Romans 8:5-6).

The Holy Spirit controls us so that we no longer find ourselves coming back to repeat the sin. We have been forgiven for our sins when we accepted Christ as our savior, but when we surrender our lives to His control, sin no longer has power over our lives. Victory (as explained in Romans seven and eight) is release from the power of sin over your life. This isn't something you do but what God does for you.

1. "He moved into you and wants to live His life through you." Spiritual rebirth is "our souls are now connected to a new power source. Christ is our new power source. He has become our life and His life is flowing in and through us" (FW Handout). "The Holy Spirit, who lives within the spirit of the believer, is controlling the personality and thus the behavior, producing the fruit of the Spirit" (*Handbook to Happiness*).

> *Victory is release from the power of sin over your life.*

2. Man is a triune being. "The spirit is the master, the soul is the servant, the body is the slave" (FW handout). The soul is the house for our mind and emotions. Our willful choices come out of our soul. Once the Holy Spirit indwells in our spirit and controls our lives, sin no longer has power over us. With the Holy Spirit as the master of our soul, we start to make willful choices that are increasingly more Christ-like. We are no longer in bondage to sin but instead a slave to the Holy Spirit and thus many sicknesses are relieved. This means the porn addict no longer is drawn to those websites; it means the adulterer is no longer drawn to contacting that

other person. Pray a prayer to have Jesus live His life through you and release you from the bondage and power of each sin in your life.

Homework: be aware this week of the Holy Spirit working in your life as you release control to Him.

The message of the CROSS and a new IDENTITY in Christ.
(Chapter 3 & 6 *The Handbook to Happiness*)

The message of the cross is dying to live. We die to our old self each day so that we have victory through our Christ controlled life (Romans 8:36-37) .

Not only did He die for us, but we died with Him. "Not only was he crucified for us but that we were crucified with Him" (*Handbook to Happiness*). We believe that we have died and been resurrect with Christ, each and every day. For example, I believe my old self lies at the bottom of the Pacific ocean where I was baptized.

Identity

Exchange our old identity for our identity in Christ—the one He had always planned for us to be, not the one we are now that has been formed through our experiences in the world. "Teaching, preaching, and discipleship can be very helpful; but in the final analysis, one's identity is first and foremost a work of the Holy Spirit" (*Handbook to Happiness*). We "live out our new and true identity in Him" (*Handbook to Happiness*). Identification—also called the exchanged Life—is

NOT intellectual identification. We are transformed into our Christ-identity after we die to our old identity—the one we thought and believed that we were, according to what the world had taught us or we had developed in reaction to the world. We accept our true identity in Christ by faith and not by works (i.e. self effort). Pray a prayer to Jesus stating your belief that you are completely new creatures in Him, with your old self as far away as a person you had know long ago but no longer know.

The Cross Experience

Brokenness is recognizing that we haven't been successful— sometimes miserably defeated—using our own plans and power. "Our path to the Cross, as well as the Cross itself, is a path of suffering, but it is the only path that leads to the end of suffering" (*The Wheel & Line* tract). "Are you willing to die to all that you are so you can live in all that He is? To do so is to exchange the self-life for the Christ-life and be filled with and controlled by the Holy Spirit. To refuse to do so is to continue a walk after the flesh and to grieve the Spirit with a continuation of conflict, suffering and defeat" (*The Wheel & Line* tract).

Total surrender means "we grant the Holy Spirit our permission to make the Cross a reality in our experience" (*Handbook to Happiness*). "Experiencing the cross is an ongoing process." "We have the choice whether to listen to and follow our emotions OR the will of God (the indwelling Christ)" (FW Handout). "Even though we have been released from the power of sin (having to obey it) by the death of our old selves, we realize that we have a choice of either 'walking in the flesh' or 'walking in the Spirit'" (adapted from *For Me to Live* booklet). We have the "choice of whether to listen to and follow our emotions OR the will of God (the indwelling Christ)" (FW Handout). Pray a prayer to Jesus stating your belief in dying on the cross with Him everyday, and your belief that to live is Christ and to die is to gain life in Him.

Homework: as you practice the cross each day, take note and journal some examples of your daily death to self and even the subsequent victory you might have experienced as a result.

The Holy Spirit TRANSFORMS our lives and RENEWS our minds and emotions.
(Chapter 5 The Handbook to Happiness)

You'll be changed from the inside out (Romans 12:1 MSG). The Lord will transform you into an image of Christ. "May God himself, the God who makes everything holy and whole, make you holy and whole, put you together—spirit, soul, and body—and keep you fit for the coming of our Master, Jesus Christ" (1 Thes. 5:23 MSG).

Spiritual regeneration happens when we accept Christ as our Savior. His Spirit lives permanently in our spirit, or indwells, and our spirit becomes one with His, much like a husband and wife become one in marriage, but unlike marriage which can be broken, He is permanently one with you. I am one with Him so I don't have to look outside myself for his will, He is in me and I am in Him. His will is achieved through His guiding and living His life through me. The more I am transformed and made Holy for his indwelling, the more my character is made Christ-like. I increasingly naturally act out

His will as I become more Christ-like. Spiritual regeneration is NOT the same as transformation by the Holy Spirit.

Transformation by the Holy Spirit

Now begins the suffering to get us to the place He wants us to be. He takes the mess we've made of our life and puts it right again, but not without a some suffering and struggle along the way. To accept His discipline we have to become teachable once again, "Conforming to the image of Christ" (Romans 8:29), through Bible study, prayer and discipleship (mentors, sermons, fellowship). "Such conformity involves suffering. The 'all things' of Romans 8:28 which work together for good are rarely seen as good in themselves, except in retrospect" (*The Wheel & Line* tract).

His transformation of our lives is an every expanding circle. He promises that He will not give us more than we can handle. Gradually He makes us submit and surrender more and more areas of our life to His loving control. We allow the Holy Spirit to do the searching within us, instead of ourselves, and reveal—according to His timing—the roots and rocks in our lives that must be removed. He will renew our minds and emotions but not through any self-effort or self-help on our parts. "We are not to become introspective and test every thought and action to see if Christ or self or satan is responsible for them. We are merely to commit the day and our life to God and trust him to control us and each situation to his glory" (*Handbook to Happiness*). Instead of waiting for signs of what His will is, we make sensible choices and at the same time allowing God to open doors (where it is His will). We look to the Lord to overcome conflicts and situations through His grace instead of through our self-effort.

Renewal of the mind is what happens when the Holy Spirit is given unconditional control of our lives.

Pastor Sumo, of Hope Chapel West Oahu, commented that goldsmiths, when smelting gold, could tell if the gold was pure if they could see their reflection in the pool of molten gold. Truly God is working on purifying us like gold so that he can see Christ's refection in us. God is purifying us for his purpose and He is making us Holy for his indwelling. It is so much more than a remodel of a home—it is a complete supernatural tranformation through death and rebirth of all

I can believe and accept Christ in my life and my spirit becomes one with His Holy Spirit, but the Holy Spirit's transformation can't really take place until I surrender completely and center my life on Him.

parts of our life and being (one by one or more at a time).

When I first surrendered and the Holy Spirit started working on me, I got a tight feeling or soreness in my brain and fuzzy thinking. I was unable to concentrate for long periods and had general body fatigue. I couldn't get any work done and everything in my life had to be put on hold. I barely had enough energy to function in my family. Even weeks later, I still felt a tightness at the top of my head and brain. It wasn't pain but it was like some wonderful transformation of my mind and brain was taking place. After surrendering my wife frequently had a headaches and couldn't read the Bible because it kept getting fuzzy. When the Holy Spirit is working on you don't try to do too much—instead of just allow him to do his work—otherwise you will over-extend yourself and feel the consequences of that, like fatigue, irritability, negativity, etc.

This process also happened when I prayed for God to take a burden off my heart. I felt the burden move to my head as a tightening on my brain. As if my brain were a cube block puzzle and God was pushing around the pieces underneath my skull. Months later I was not incapacitated but God was still working on me, showing me my inner vows that I must break and areas I must submit to His Lordship. Later, God began to convict me in smaller matters, like erasing the pirated software and music on my computer. And after that, He began to disciple me: teaching me not to place trust in situations or things but only in Him; teaching me to respond to life's situations in an adult manner instead of reacting like a child. He has also grown a greater faith in me—in His providing for my needs and my commitment to tithe.

Renewal of the mind and healing of emotions will eventually change the way you "feel" about things. "The Holy Spirit is the real therapist if we allow Him to work through us" (FW Handout). All the expressions of sin (inferiority, depression, etc.) that come out of defeat are healed as God transforms our lives and renews our minds. The Lord (not through your actions or works) will make you a mature Christian—which is the image of Christ. "Unlike the culture around you, always dragging you down to its level of immaturity, God brings the best out of you, develops well-formed maturity in you" (Romans 12:1 MSG).

Homework: What is your experience now that you have surrendered? Did you notice any signs of transformation and renewal? If not, that doesn't mean you haven't surrendered—transformation and renewal is according to God's timing and ways.

The VICTORY in Christ experience.
(Chapter 7 *The Handbook to Happiness*)

Many people tell me it's not possible to know whether someone is victorious in Christ or not, but Pastor Sumo pointed out all you have to do is look at the fruit. I agree, the proof is in the fruit, victorious lives produce spiritual fruit: love, joy, peace, patience, kindness, goodness, faithfulness, gentleness, and self-control. Spiritual fruit isn't produced through self-effort but through the walking in the Holy Spirit—which is the

> *Victorious lives produce spiritual fruit.*

essence of a victorious life. Victory is the loss of self, identity and control leading to a totally dependent relationship on Him. We die to our old selves for a new life in Him. We die to our old identity for a new identity in Christ, and we release control of our lives to the Holy Spirit. Remember, we don't seek the fruit or victory but instead seek God and the rest will follow.

Another sign of a victorious life is what comes out of our mouths—as many of the Bible's proverbs point out. What you say flows from what is in your heart (Luke 6:45). Inferiority/

superiority complexes and unresolved inner conflicts are signs of someone who hasn't claimed their victory in Christ, because these begin to fade as we are healed through walking in the Spirit.

Walking in the Spirit vs Walking in the Flesh

"For every child of God defeats this evil world, and we achieve this victory through our faith. And who can win this battle against the world? Only those who believe that Jesus is the Son of God" (John 5:4-5).

"The problem of walking in defeat is not that we don't have victory (because we have been set free, and Christ's life is victorious in us for whatever we face). But we can choose (consciously or subconsciously) not to claim our victory and continue to live as though we're in bondage. This condition of our lives is called 'walking after the flesh' rather than 'walking after the Spirit'. The world says we attain victory by doing; God says we obtain it by dying or counting ourselves dead to sin. It is exactly backwards from our world system training; the way up is down; we have to fail in order to succeed; we have to die in order to live" (*For Me to Live* booklet).

Characteristics of the self life (walking in the flesh):

Stubbornness, Vanity, Pride, Inferiority Feelings, Bigotry, Egoism, Selfish Ambition, Impatience, Envy, Hypersensitivity, Withdrawal, Dissension, Loveless, Anxiety, Guilt, False Modesty, Fear, Self Justification, Indifference, Self Indulgence, Dominance, Self Reliance, Critical Spirit, Self Effort, Depression, Self Righteousness, Nervousness, Laziness, Hostility, and Anger (*For Me to Live* booklet).

"Let the Holy Spirit guide your lives" (Gal. 5:16). Walking in the Spirit means "Christ is in control of you." "If we make decisions based on our feelings and emotions" we are walking in the flesh. "As long as we do not act according to our emotions and wrong thoughts and instead make our decisions based on the Word of God, we are in the Spirit." (FW Handout). "Once the Holy Spirit has illuminated the truth of our death and resurrection with Christ and it is an experiential reality, we must continue to walk in the spirit, denying ourselves and taking up the cross daily" (Luke 9:23) (*Handbook to Happiness*). Abide in Christ (John 15:5). Abide means to live, dwell, accept or act in accordance with. "This is a lifelong process, during which a person encounters spiritual warfare and the flesh must daily be brought to nothing" (*Handbook to Happiness*).

God's voice can be like the alarm clock in the morning telling me to get up but my body doesn't want to. I have to ignore what my body, emotions, and thoughts are telling me and push myself to do what God Spirit is leading me to do.

UPS and DOWNS

There are ups and downs in the victorious life. The first thing that happened to the Israelites after their first victory (after crossing the Jordan) was defeat. They had to turn to God and ask Him to point out where they went wrong, and as soon as they found the sin they had committed and repented of it, they were on to victory again. A downer starts with negativity, worry, frustration, evolving into anger and depression, and trying to do things ourselves (*Handbook to Happiness*). It's a feeling like we aren't in contact with God anymore; forgetting all that He has already done for us and questioning whether He exists or cares. We've lost our joy and "aren't singing in the shower" anymore. We don't know where, when or how it happened, but it did. We have to turn to prayer, fasting and fellowship for support; drop whatever we're doing and open our Bibles. It is amazing how I can be in a downer, feeding my face, feeling numb, and then drag myself to mini-church and suddenly by the middle of the evening I am filled with the Spirit.

Jason Lehfeldt's strategic prayer (see chapter 3) can also be helpful to find the blockage or wedge in our relationships that is causing our disconnection with God, ourselves and others. We confess and repent of our sins, God cleanses us, and we continue to walk in the Spirit having faith in our position and our (already finished) victory in Christ. "The blood never loses it's power to cleanse and restore" (*Handbook to Happiness*). We are always righteous (in right standing with God) because of Christ's sacrifice and not because of anything we do today or tomorrow.

Through a series of ups and downs the Holy Spirit shows us the areas of our lives and souls that are prone to sin or self and we begin to be healed and understand how to bounce back into victory faster and longer. Be careful to work from victory instead of for victory. Walking in the Spirit goes from being a day to day experience to a moment by moment experience. No part of our lives are too small or too insignificant to submit to the Lord and seek His counsel. No moment is too small to seek His will for

> *Be careful to work from victory instead of for victory.*

that moment. "The Lord directs the steps of the godly. He delights in every detail of their lives. Though they stumble, they will never fall, for the Lord holds them by the hand" (Psalm 37:23-24). It takes work to spiritually mature and accept God's discipline and discipleship, but never fall into the trap of thinking we have to work for victory. Grace is unmerited favor and unconditional love. We receive his grace not by doing things (works or performance) but just by having faith in Him and that we are already victorious in Him, and the battle has already been won.

THOUGHTS and EMOTIONS

We live in a fallen world and the enemy and our sinful nature may attack our thoughts and emotions. We combat this by casting all our thoughts upon Christ, laying all our burdens at His feet. We feel like dying! So why not die to live?

We can base our decisions and better discern His will for our thoughts and emotions through constant Bible reading. I started with the New Testament and read it from the beginning to the end in about four months, reading a few pages a day and meditating on it, NOT speed-reading, not reading for intellectual 'knowledge', but instead opening myself to what the Holy Spirit wanted to show me. Read Romans at least twice. After reading the New Testament, I received a copy of the Daily Bible and started reading it from the beginning. The Old Testament helped me to understand the nature and character of God, whereas the new testament taught me about love and grace. The Daily Bible is extremely helpful in understanding the Old Testament because it is chronologically arranged and has many commentaries that explain a passage's significance—giving a deeper understanding that would have been lost on me otherwise.

"We cannot always believe our emotions! They may have been 'damaged' as a result of the 'programming' of the old life. We may be 'feeling' good (e.g. I Corinthians 10:12), without being in fellowship with God, even if things 'seem well' (my note—many non-Christians and carnal Christians are good examples of this). The contrary is also true: times of trial—when everything seems to go wrong—can be times of real faith and dependence upon God (II Corinthians 4:7-11), but our feelings may tell us things are not going well. If, by faith, we claim Christ to be our Life—His Living Life through us—then His Life, His Character, His Fruit, will be ours in experience (Soul) only as we are conformed to the reality of His Life in our Spirit" (*For Me to Live* booklet).

(End of *The Handbook to Happiness* study guide)

3

Spiritual Warfare

Fighting in the Spirit instead of the flesh.

For we are not fighting against flesh-and-blood enemies, but against evil rulers and authorities of the unseen world, against mighty powers in this dark world, and against evil spirits in the heavenly places (Ephesians 6:12). We are human, but we don't wage war as humans do. We use God's mighty weapons, not worldly weapons, to knock down the strongholds of human reasoning and to destroy false arguments (2 Corinthians 10:3-5).

The enemy's only weapon is deception. Victory is always ours, just like forgiveness only takes one time, we don't lose victory after we have gained it—although our sinful nature and the enemy will try to deceive us into thinking we've lost our victory or haven't really forgiven. We can combat the deceptions of the enemy through speaking and replying with scriptures we have memorized. The scripture is the Word of God and more powerful than the enemy or any self defense we can muster. God's commands, covenants and promises are an effective sword against the enemy.

Don't fight people but instead recognize it's a spiritual warfare. The evil we see or sense in others is only overcome through God's power. Pray, read the Bible, and answer questions with scripture. Instead of getting into a control battle, surrender the situation to God—die to live. Let God show you, in you, what is causing the conflict. Release the other person, let God do the work in the other person according to His way and timing. Not only pray for those that we love but also those that we don't love. Pray for God's blessing on their relationship with God.

Distance from God

The Psalms are examples of David having times of feeling distance from God. It's good to read the Psalms during personal trials. In one chapter David is praising God: "I prayed to the Lord, and he answered me, He freed me from all my fears" (Psalm 34:4); and in the next he asking, "How long, O Lord, will you look on and do nothing?" (Psalm 35:17).

Read the Psalms during personal trials.

Pastor Don Cousins gave a sermon at HCWO and explained we are to pray fervently during those 'Where are you God?' moments. The results of fervent prayer can be one of three things:

1. God changes our circumstances. For example, He gives a better job, heals us, brings our child back to Christianity, etc. In the book of Acts, the people praying for Peter were probably hoping that Herod would change His mind and not

execute Peter. They weren't prepared for God to answer their prayer in the way that He did, by having an angel release Peter from prison and Peter come directly to their home. Just like the people praying for Peter, we must keep praying but keep an open mind.

2. God reveals His purposes. He opens our eyes to why we are in these circumstances. In the case of Paul, in spite of fervent prayer, God kept the thorn in Paul's side, because in Paul's weakness God's power is perfected. He shows us that what we are going through has a purpose. We didn't understand the lesson and now we do, or we didn't understand where the path led but now He has shown us.

3. God strengthens our spirit. God strengthens us to the point we are examples to others, and inspire other's faith, for example, an ongoing battle with cancer.

Strategic Praying

Lay Pastor Jason Lehfeldt of Mountain View Community Church in Kaneohe has a four step process of strategic prayer.

Jason demonstrated with the above diagram that if there is a wedge in any of these relationships (with others, God or yourself) it will create a wedge in all of them. He uses the four following steps to remove these wedges:

1. Repent - "Now repent of your sins and turn to God, so that your sins may be wiped away." (Acts 3:19)

If he isn't singing songs of praise in the shower, or whenever he loses peace, he sits down on the couch and prays, "God what are you trying to show me, in me?" He will keep praying until it is revealed to him; he will ask God just for a small flag to show him where he has gone wrong so that he can repent and submit to God.

2. Renounce

This step was new to me but is one of the most powerful parts of this strategy. After repenting we must renounce, disown, and dislodge the lies about ourselves and others that remain in our thoughts such as: labels of others; our 'rights' and what we think we 'deserve'; and any stories in our head making another person the villain.

We say to ourselves "I don't deserve to be treated like..." We demand our rights but what we have is a right to forgive. Recognize that they are just another hurting person and lift them up in prayer instead of getting bent about it. We all have expectations and standards of love, honor, respect, etc. Holding others to our standards is killing our relationships and we are losing our peace. For example, like our expectation of people being on time. We need to communicate our feelings and ask they just give us a call. We can't let our expectations control our life.

3. Forgive

After repenting and renouncing then we forgive ourselves and others. We keep praying through to forgiveness, peeling the layers, and persevering until we "return to a place of feeling compassion for them." We don't need to hold anyone responsible, accountable, or punish them—let God do that work. For strategic praying, "we are led by the Spirit and not feelings. I am willing even if I don't feel like it." We can also pray "God help me to get to a place I can forgive."

"God's plan is to build our character and spiritual fighting skills—not get us to a comfortable place." We are to be as wise as serpents and as gentle as doves. We must keep wise and healthy boundaries. If someone keeps sinning against us, we must forgive but we don't have go back to a situation if they keep hurting us. Maybe someday we'll be healthy enough or they will grow. You don't have to put yourself back on the firing line.

4. Rebuke

Lastly, we rebuke any evil—but this may not be necessary because when you submit to God, satan will flee. "If you get rid of the garbage the rats will leave." Through completing these steps we "release the healing and restoring of the Holy Spirit." For Jason prayer is more about submitting and repenting than rebuking the devil. We can have thoughts that are from our sinful nature that are not necessarily a fiery dart from an evil spirit or the devil.

"Do not judge others, and you will not be judged. For you will be treated as you treat others. The standard you use in judging is the standard by which you will be judged." (Matthew 7:1) Judgement is the sin of being critical of and condemning others. Discernment is not judgement, it longs to see restoration and is not critical. There are a lot of imperfect people out there and a word of correction has to be out of love. We are here to help and see them restored instead of condemning. Jason says there are times when he had to pray for two weeks before he was in right frame of mind to approach someone with love instead of condemnation.

He used a ruler in his presentation to signify how were constantly holding it up and measuring others against our expectations and at the end of the seminar he broke it symbolizing what we must do in our own lives.

Trials and Transformation.

But consider the joy of those corrected by God!
Do not despise the discipline of the Almighty
when you sin.
For though he wounds, he also bandages.
He strikes, but his hands also heal.
(Job 5:17-18)

We receive (sometimes very painful) correction from God for our sins. God exiled the Israelites to Babylon for seventy years. He wanted them to turn their heart back to Him, to obey His voice, and love Him with all their heart. Afterwards, He changed their circumstances by freeing them to go back to Israel and be blessed again.

Or a man may be chastened on a bed of pain
with constant distress in his bones,
so that his very being finds food repulsive
and his soul loathes the choicest meal.
(Job 33:19-20)

If God doesn't answer our pleading prayers it's because He has a greater plan in mind, one that will transform us with the refining fire of the Holy Spirit. For many years I rejected the church, and hardened my heart toward Christians, but still prayed and pleaded to God. God would not answer because there was still farther hardship and destruction that had to take place in my life before I would finally surrender and open my heart to Christ and His church. It wasn't a plan of punishment or one to give me greater patience and endurance—it was a plan of complete transformation. If by some superhuman feat I had just patiently (or more-like painfully) endured I would never have made the change He was calling me to make. Fortunately, instead, I was broken, and in that brokenness He saved and transformed me.

> *Many fear looking at their inner self because of what they might find, and what God might ask them to change.*

Shall we accept good from God, and not trouble?
(Job 2:10)

Job is an example that suffering isn't always a result of sin. God wants to know whether your faith is contingent on the well-being of your family, physical health, and financial status. Suffering is God's way of calling us into a closer relationship with Him through deeper levels of surrender, obedience, faith, and inner healing.

Many fear looking at their inner self because of what they might find, and what God might ask them to change. Inner work is usually more painful than just enduring and developing patience with our current circumstances. God is the one who does the searching and exposing of the areas (both inward than outward) that He wants us to look at, pray about, and release to His Lordship. He wants to set us free from bondage—through faith in His healing grace (i.e. supernatural power). This usually starts with us dying to and/or surrendering parts of ourselves. We must willingly choose to take an inner journey: to look inward at the past rejection and hurt (from society and family), generational sin, inequities, inner vows, inner bondage, lack of balance, and repressed parts of ourselves.

For God speaks again and again,
though people do not recognize it.
He speaks in dreams, in visions of the night,
when deep sleep falls on people
as they lie in their beds.
He whispers in their ears
and terrifies them with warnings.
He makes them turn from doing wrong;
he keeps them from pride.
He protects them from the grave,
from crossing over the river of death.
(Job 33:14-18)

A lot of inner work is unconscious work. Dreams are the place where God speaks to our waking self about the parts of ourselves we aren't aware of. Of course, He can still get the message to us through a million other miraculous means, but He does like to use dreams (in the Bible and in my life). Whether you decide to listen to your dreams or not, God wants to do some inner refining work in you. Inner transformation is a much more difficult road but also more spiritually rewarding. Gifts of the Holy Spirit, blessings and joy in our lives, and the fruit of the Holy Spirit are all spiritual rewards of a victorious life in Christ.

> *A lot of inner work is unconscious work.*

4

The Holy Spirit

Jesus told the parable of the farmer scattering seed:

> And other fell on good ground, and did yield fruit that sprang up and increased; and brought forth, some thirty, and some sixty, and some an hundred. (Mark 4:8)

Pastor Max Solbrekken said, 'Jesus places believers in three categories: thirty percent, sixty percent and one hundred percent! The famous American Evangelist, D.L. Moody said: "The first class, are those who got to Calvary and there got life. They believed on the Son and were saved, and there they rested satisfied. They did not seek anything higher. You might safely say, I think, without exaggeration, that 19 out of 20 Christians...have just got life and have settled down, and have not sought for power."

The second class, Moody called, "a better class of Christian," asserting, "the secret of the Holy Spirit's coming in power to the believer is the individual's complete surrender to the Saviour. And we do not need to wait upon God to do something for us. He is waiting for us to yield ourselves to Him."

Moody pointed to John 7:37,38: "out of whose belly (innermost being) shall flow rivers of living water." He said, "This is the best class; this is the kind of Christian we ought to be."

So what is this living water? Jesus Promises Living Water. On the last day, the climax of the festival, Jesus stood and shouted to the crowds, "Anyone who is thirsty may come to me! Anyone who believes in me may come and drink! For the Scriptures declare, 'Rivers of living water will flow from his heart.'" (When he said "living water," he was speaking of the Spirit, who would be given to everyone believing in him. But the Spirit had not yet been given, because Jesus had not yet entered into his glory) (John 7:37,38). The living water is His Holy Spirit.

Christian faith is threefold just like the Holy Trinity (Father, Son, and Holy Spirit), the triune of man (spirit, soul, and body), and the triune of a marriage (God, husband, and wife). We are thirty percent Christian after accepting Christ (we believe that Jesus is our Savior and died for our sins, thus we are reborn or regenerated); then become sixty percent Christian when we completely surrender our lives to Christ; and we become one hundred percent Christian after were baptized by the Holy Spirit. This, of course, doesn't imply anything about whether your saved, going to heaven or have eternal life (we'll leave that debate for the theologians). The important thing to remember is that there is a fuller life possible as a Christian.

Charles Solomon says there are "three basic junctures of salvation, total surrender, and identification". John

Wesley, the father of the Methodist church and Pentecostal movement, calls the first step (the thirty percent Christians), "the ones who are saved— justified—but have not yet received the new, clean heart. They have received forgiveness through the blood of Christ, but have not received the constant indwelling of the Holy Spirit." The second step is complete surrender. We must desire His Spirit so greatly that we are willing to sell or lose all that we

> *We must desire His Spirit so greatly that we are willing to sell or lose all that we have and die to our old selves (future plans, worldly desires, etc.) to live in Christ.*

have and die to our old selves (future plans, worldly desires, etc.) to live in Christ. We can't reach the third step unless we take the first and second steps. There are several terms used for this last step to one hundred percent Christian: identification, exchanged life, victorious living, baptism of the Holy Spirit, revival, filling of the Spirit, living faith, indwelling of the Holy Spirit, outpouring of the Holy Spirit, etc.

Baptism of the Holy Spirit

Baptism also is threefold (just like he three junctures of Christian faith). Pastor Max Sobrekken says, "First, when we are born again, we are baptized into the Body of Christ by the Holy Spirit (Gal. 3:27). Secondly, there is the believer's baptism in water, by immersion (Mark 16:16, Acts 2:41), and thirdly, there is the 'Baptism in the Holy Ghost and Fire' by Jesus Christ Himself (Luke 3:16)."

Baptism of the Holy Spirit is not the same thing as a water baptism. Water baptism can be like a celebration while baptism of the Holy Spirit can be like a wave of release, peace, and tears of joy. Water baptism is a declaration of faith and a cleansing that prepares us for the Baptism of the Holy Spirit, but is not necessary for the baptism of the Holy Spirit. I was water baptized two months after experiencing baptism of the Holy Spirit. Peter (Acts 10:44-48) water baptized the house of Cornelius after they had received baptism of the Holy Spirit (evidenced by their speaking in tongues). One practice of the early church was to lay hands on someone (and pray) after water baptism so that they would receive the baptism of the Holy Spirit.

If you've been baptized by the Holy Spirit you would know it.

Pastor Jonathan Goforth said if you've been baptized by the Holy Spirit you would know it. Solbrekken says the only outward sign, according to the Bible, is that you will speak in tongues, prophesy, and magnify (extol and glorify) God. Pastor Ray Brubaker was physically healed after experiencing the baptism of the Holy Spirit. Joyce Meyer heard God's voice. The biggest sign of all is that the power of sin is broken (victory over sin). During my baptism of the Holy Spirit, I felt a rush over my body, the tears of relief streamed down my face, and subsequently the power of sin was broken (porn addiction, obsession, etc.).

HOW does the Holy Spirit come upon you? In many ways. Some through the laying on of hands (with prayer)—as in the Bible. We pray to accept Christ as our Savior and we must pray to receive His Spirit. It is a "definite experience subsequent to conversion".

When the apostles in Jerusalem heard that the people of Samaria had accepted God's message, they sent Peter and John there. As soon as they arrived, they prayed for these new believers to receive the Holy Spirit. The Holy Spirit had not yet come upon any of them, for they had only been baptized in the name of the Lord Jesus. Then Peter and John laid their hands upon these believers, and they received the Holy Spirit (Acts 8:14-17).

All we have to do is ask for it and God will give it to us. Trumbull, author of *Victory in Christ*, spent years as a defeated Christian, then he read a sermon on 'For me to live is Christ', prayed to God and finally experienced victory. Brubaker said he went to a Baptism of the Spirit service at church and was prayed for and touched by the minister but nothing happened. Then after four days of prayer and fasting the Spirit came upon him at night. Dr. Solomon prayed for counseling clients in his office and the Spirit immediately was poured into them. I accepted Christ when I was thirteen, but I felt the outpouring of the Holy Spirit when I read Solomon's book last year. John Wesley continuously sought this living faith "though with some strange indifference, dullness, and coldness". Then one day, he "was listening to a reading of Luther's preface to the Epistle to the Romans. While he was describing the change which God works in the heart through faith in Christ, I felt my heart strangely warmed. I felt that I did trust in Christ, Christ alone for salvation. An assurance was given me that He had taken away my sins, even mine, and saved me from the law of sin and death." Joyce Meyer "cried out to God...telling Him something was missing in my relationship with Him. I heard the audible voice of God the day I was filled with the Holy Spirit...and I was suddenly filled with faith that He was going to do something wonderful in my life."

Our Pentecostal church has hosted pastors from our denomination, such as Leslie Keegal (from Sri Lanka) and Lanil Gunasekara (from Australia) for healing services. We had a Holy Spirit night of worship and sermon, then afterwards the pastor called up people who wanted to receive baptism of the Holy Spirit or healing. The minister and sometimes others who possessed the spiritual gift of healing would lay hands on the person, pray and then after a moment the minister would put the palm of his hand on their forehead and push them backwards into the waiting arms of others who would lay them on the floor. Some call this being 'slain in the spirit'. They fall on their back being overwhelmed by the Holy Spirit or others just want to trust God and let go. Some people will do this on more than one occasion to receive another filling of the Holy Spirit—at times of renewing faith and coming back into repentance—while others wish to be 'slain' more than once for an ongoing illness. It's a matter of how we feel led by the Holy Spirit. This kind of service is also frequently done at church retreats.

WHEN does baptism of the Holy Spirit happen? Only John the Baptist was filled with the Holy Spirit from birth (Luke 1:15). If you read the book of Acts you will find many are subsequent to conversion. It took Saul/Paul in the Bible three days from conversion. Some people are converted and spend a long time in the wilderness (in the world) and are baptized with the Holy Spirit later in life, but it can happen any time according to God's plan. I accepted Christ at thirteen and it was twenty five years before I experienced it (I didn't know about surrender and baptism of the Holy Spirit before that). Trumbull and Wesley were Christian pastors for several years before experiencing it. For many of Solomon's counseling clients it was instantaneous after he explained it to them and they prayed together for it. Joyce Meyer spent many years going to church before finally fully submitting her life to Christ and becoming victorious through baptism of the Holy Spirit.

WHY do we need it? To break the power of sin in our lives and to receive our spiritual gifts and the power and authority of the Holy Spirit. The indwelling Holy Spirit purifies and cleanses our conscience (inner voice and common sense). Victorious lives reap the fruit of the Holy Spirit: love, joy, peace, patience, kindness, goodness, faithfulness, gentleness, and self-control. After Jesus was baptized (in the water) he prayed and the Holy Spirit descended on Him. "If the Son of God has got to be anointed, do not his disciples need it, and shall we not seek it, and shall we barely rest with conversion?" (D.L Moody).

Holy Spirit renewal and transformation

Positive thinking and self-help are methods of deception used by the enemy. None of these things make us better; psychology can help us understand ourselves but only God has the power to heal and transform us.

We can try to change the way we think and act through self-effort but only the Holy Spirit can truly transform us. This is a process called 'dying to live'. Each day we choose to die to our old selves and way of thinking and give God complete control over our lives.

Renewal of the mind is not a process of self-effort, but instead of one of surrender. Renewal occurs through the grace (supernatural power) of God. Reading the Bible, listening to sermons, and being discipled by others, are all tools the Holy Spirit uses for us to die to our old way of thinking and be reborn into a Christ-like character.

I can be a Bible intellectual and still not experience the cross.

Don't be fooled into thinking this is as intellectually achieved renewal instead of a miracle of the Holy Spirit. I can be a Bible intellectual and still not experience the cross of dying to my old self (and its way of thinking); it's through resurrection into a new life in Christ that this internal change happens.

The indwelling of the Holy Spirit is the underlying supernatural force that increasingly takes parts of our lives and transforms them into a Christ-like character. The Holy Spirit drives and heals the soul, which is the seat for our thoughts, emotions and will. Out of our soul comes our behaviors (functional or dysfunctional) and physical reactions (healthy or sick).

If we are centered on self, instead of God, then we are not surrendered to the Holy Spirit renewal of our minds and transformation of our emotions. If we are self-willed we will continue to make bad choices, use mental escapes (e.g. obsessiveness), experience emotions like chronic depression and anxiety, and have physical reactions (e.g. stomachaches, skin problems, etc).

Renewal of the mind.

It's not a sin to have thoughts and emotions, but what we choose to do with them can lead to sin: either through dwelling on them or making the wrong choice on how to act on them. We should cast all our thoughts (and emotions) upon Christ. He will transform us so that we don't have that thought or emotion anymore, or He will guide us in our decision on how to act on that thought or emotion. God may also use that bit of suffering, that results from a re-occurring thought or emotion, as an ongoing catalyst for us to continue to rely on and turn to Him.

Jimmy Evans, in a recent television interview, said the Bible is a two edged sword, one side for using against the enemy and the other a scalpel used for the renewal of our mind. We memorize, ponder and meditate on the Bible and it renews our mind. We combat attacks—thoughts from the enemy—by recalling scriptures we have memorized, because God and his Word are more powerful than any thought or attack from the enemy.

The Hero of the Bible

I finished (for the first time but not the last) the most life-changing book I have ever read. The hero of the story is the most incredible person who ever walked the earth. God is the hero of the Bible. Lori Salierno (of Celebrate Life International) said God was:

Adam's redeemer
Eve's tree of life
Abel's vindication
Noah's ark
Abraham's sacrifice
Isaac's hope
Judah's shiloh
Gideon's captain
Mose's rock
Joshua's courage
Deborah's zeal
Samson's strength
Elijah's fire
Samuel's Ebenezer
Isaiah's Prince of Peace
Jeremiah's balm
Hosea's love
Micah's mercy
Amos' justice
David's music
Solomon's wisdom

Reading the Bible cleared up many of the misconceptions
I had about God's character, integrity, and how He operates
in our lives. How can you know a person without learning
about their history—it's the same with God! There are
misconceptions about God that we learn through our culture
(especially movies that misinterpret or fictionalize the Bible),
and even from the limited perspective of simple Bible stories

taught in Sunday school. I started out by reading the New Testament. It was an incredible awakening to the fact that I had been living and believing in a relationship with God based on the Old Testament instead the new covenant of grace by faith and not by works. Then I move onto the Old Testament and found out how God really is the hero of the story and the Rock of every well-known name in the Bible. I learn how the Israelites didn't have it made once they reached the promise land—they had to destroy the people that lived in it first. And a thousand years later they still didn't have it made when God brought them out of exile from Babylon—they had to face enemy nations as they rebuilt God's temple, their city, and the walls of Jerusalem. I learned how even God's chosen people, in the face of impossible circumstances, had to always move forward trusting in Him.

Why read the Bible

I constantly searched through bookstores and libraries but only found books filled with blank pages until I opened the Bible last year. The searching ended. I wasn't looking for the right words on the page, I was looking for something that spoke to my starving spirit. When I had read the Bible with a closed heart the Holy Spirit couldn't speak to my spirit, but after I opened my heart to Jesus, His Holy Spirit spoke through verse after verse in His word.

One big reason to read the Bible is that many Christian books quote scripture but we don't really get the deeper meaning of those quotes without having read the full book in the Bible. I used to read Bible quotes in books by various Christian authors and I always got the feeling like when you read a novel and there is a break in the story or a change in the voice of the speaker that upsets the continuity. Read the whole Bible first, then as we read Christian books those scriptures echo what the Holy Spirit has taught us—instead of one authors interpretation of a few lines in the Bible. I recommend the Daily Bible. It has a chronological arrangement which makes it easier to follow.

Lastly, as you read the Bible you will find yourself searching for scriptures on certain topics. The concordance in the back of the Bible is handy but don't be fooled into believing it contains every occurrence of a word in the Bible. For example, if you want to see every occurrence of the word 'dream' my NLT version has only two listings, but the online version of the NLT will give you every listing (113 total). I recommend this website for searching the Bible:

http://bibleresources.bible.com/passagesearch.php

And to search the Bible in other languages:

http://unbound.biola.edu

The word of God the sword of the Spirit (Ephesians 6:17). For the word of God is quick, and powerful, and sharper than any two edged sword, piercing even to the dividing asunder of soul and spirit, and of the joints and marrow, and is a discerner of the thoughts and intents of the heart. (Hebrews 4:12).

Spiritual gifts and fruits of the Holy Spirit.

We can seek to develop our spiritual gifts but we shouldn't seek the fruits of the Holy Spirit. Fruits are the result of a life centered on and surrendered to the Lord's will and open to the Holy Spirit's transformation. The fruits of the Holy Spirit can be experienced on conversion but aren't lasting until we truly 'die to live' each day. The Holy Spirit produces this kind of fruit in our lives: love, joy, peace, patience, kindness, goodness, faithfulness, gentleness, and self-control. (Galatians 5:22-23)

Gifts of the Holy Spirit:

There are many passages in the bible that mention the gifts of the Holy Spirit. Here is a list I compiled from several tests and books (such as *Finding Your Spiritual Gifts Questionnaire*, and *S.H.A.P.E*). They generally have the same list of gifts with only a few different or by different titles:

Administration, apostleship or missionary, celibacy, compassion or mercy, encouragement, discernment (of spirits), evangelism, exhortation, exorcism, faith, giving, healing, helping or assisting, hospitality, interpretation (of tongues), knowledge, leadership, miracles, pastoring, prophecy, intercessory prayer, serving, teaching, tongues, voluntary poverty, and wisdom.

I didn't have to 'die to live' to experience the gifts of the Holy Spirit. I accepted Christ when I was thirteen so I can't really say whether my gifts were present before I believed in God. But my gifts of apostleship, faith, and discernment were in evidence during my twenty-five years in the wilderness. The difference is that those gifts were not truly blessed until I did 'die to live' by surrendering my whole life to His Lordship. For example, my discernment is no longer a muddy, distant, quiet, yearning feeling that I can't describe; it's now a very clear and present gift in my life—especially the more I read the Bible.

I've studied personality type in depth (I'm a Myers Briggs Qualified Practitioner), so it's not surprising that I would also take an interest in spiritual gifts. I have taken three different spiritual gifts tests and my results (in order of strength and greatest area of passion) are:

1. Apostleship - these are missionaries, but it's also the gift of creating new ministries within churches, and the gift of writing (epistles).

Many people don't realize that the apostleship gift includes writing. When I'm fasting (more than a single day) God really blesses my writing with loads of inspiration. An apostle can be a pioneering supporter of new ideas or a cause; for example, I like to write and talk about economic inequality. We can be apostles and missionaries to our workplaces and even to our churches. For this reason, I felt called to share the message of the cross and other books at my church through group study. Lastly, my book business is largely internet based and I see myself as a Christian missionary assigned to the foreign post known as the Internet.

2. Faith - unshakeable trust and confidence in God.

I've always been a sucker for leaps of faith. In my twenties, I went to live in Japan with only $900 bucks in my pocket and didn't know a soul. I love stories about, and resonate with, great men of faith. Similar to missionaries, such as Verwey and Hudson, as an author I have to trust in the Lord to provide for our needs. Recently, I'm taking a leap of faith through giving the Lord complete control and responsibility for our finances.

3. Discernment - recognize what is or is not of God.

I find it hard NOT to read other people: sensing their inconsistencies, motives, and spiritual needs. I tend to be a spiritual catalyst in other's lives and I also use this gift for spiritual warfare. This is a gift I sometimes wish I could turn off. I have to be very careful of the pitfalls of being judgmental and speaking the truth where I should just be quiet and show love instead.

At first, I made the mistake of thinking discernment is the ability to tell if the Holy Spirit is present. For example, the gift of discernment can tell me if a pastor or what he is saying is inconsistent with God's truth, but I am not able to tell whether the Holy Spirit is working through his sermon and touching people. Additionally, anyone can feel moved by the Holy Spirit during a sermon without possessing the gift of discernment.

4. Wisdom - insight and judgement into how to apply Bible scriptures in everyday life.

I use my gift of wisdom in my writing to apply spiritual truths to real life examples (like in this book). I resonate with many books by pastoral counselors (e.g. Chapman, Evans, and Lewis), who are good at applying Biblical truth and Christian values to marriage, work, and everyday life.

5. Miracles - call on God for supernatural acts that glorify Him.

This is the only gift I tend to wonder about. It still remains to be seen if I have this gift. So far I've seen miracles in my marriage. I've also noticed recently that God has been calling me to increase my faith in miracle healings.

Led by the Holy Spirit gifts

At our church we had a seminar on spiritual gifts and the pastor pointed out that the gifts of the Holy Spirit are usually not our natural talents and abilities. If we are living in victory through Christ, He will bless our talents and abilities, but He will also give us spiritual gifts in addition to that. These spiritual gifts are ones He gives us to bless others and our church with. These gifts are the Holy Spirit doing work that normally wouldn't be possible for us using our our natural talents and abilities. It's a work of the Holy Spirit making possible through God what is not possible through man.

Spiritual gifts tests might show our personality type instead of how God has chosen to work through us.

This also puts the spiritual gifts tests in question because they tend to ask questions like a personality test and thus give us indications of our nature or character instead of indications of how God has chosen to work through us. The pastor suggested you look to others to tell you your spiritual gifts. Other Christians are better at seeing what you are doing successfully—that seems to be outside your natural talents and abilities. One example is a Christian woman who never thought she was good at prayer but others told her she was. She found she was led to become part of the prayer team and God anointed that work by beginning to show her the roots (of inner work) that need to be addressed in her life because to do effective intercessory prayer you must remove the hindering things in your own life.

Your spouse may be able to see your spiritual gifts more clearly than you do. My wife suggested I have the missionary gift because I grew up in Colorado not being exposed to any other cultures, people, or languages. She sees me shine when I talk to people from other cultures and frequently make friends with them. Another indicator might be that I don't have a natural ability with foreign language. I have tried to master my wife's language (Japanese) for years with limited return compared to the effort I put in. On the other hand, I do enjoy other cultures: travel, culture differences, and foreign culture (food, religion, language, history, geography). I speculate another test of a spiritual gift is that if you don't use the gift out of love it's probably not one of the Spirit. For example, if I use my gift of wisdom in a critical and judgmental way then possibly it's not my gift after all—just an ability I use in a negative way?

Spiritual gifts won't be released until we "are delivered of the spirit of fear concerning them" (*Echoes from Heaven: Living Waters Flow*). For example, someone might feel unsure about the gift of tongues, wondering if its just something people fake. Much like dream interpretation we must be led by the Holy Spirit for indications of our spiritual gifts. Dream dictionaries can give you several ideas of what a dream symbol means but only the Holy Spirit can tell you which one fits your life and the message God is trying to convey to you. The same with spiritual gift tests, they can educate you on the different spiritual gifts, through definitions, check off lists, and roles they play in the church, but the Holy Spirit using you for a particular gift is the TRUE indicator.

My wife also thinks I might have the gifts of healing, word of knowledge, administration, and mercy. I can tell you that administration is definitely not a natural ability and even torments me, but if God gifts me in this capacity I will experience an anointing that will surpass any of my limitations. As for healing, I've always been a bit put off by the likes of Benny Hinn, but on the other hand I really believe in healing of addiction, and other soul problems (mental and emotional). As an introverted intuitive type I don't worry myself much with the physical world and thus physical healing has been completely off my radar screen and not an interest of mine. But then there was one time in our mini-church that we all laid hands on someone about to get back surgery and I felt an immense presence of the Holy Spirit working through me. Then there was another time where I felt a great burden to have our mini-church pray for a fellow church member's healing, and when I started the prayer I was brought to tears by the power present. Lastly, I went to a Holy Spirit Night (at our church) and many people lay 'slain in the spirit' on the floor; I had my hands raised up to God but felt moved to turn them toward the people on the floor and I felt my arms and hands being moved side to side with His power.

Maybe spiritual gifts correlate with the love languages. Gary Chapman in his book, *The Love Languages of God*, explained that the touch love language type will raise their hands to feel God's presence. One example was a man's hands would tremble when he prayed with others. My love language is touch and my hands have trembled in the past when I was in prayer groups. This is God's way of showing me

His love and power through my love language, in addition to my spiritual gifts.

5

Christian Dream Interpretation

And the Lord said to them, "Now listen to what I say: "If there were prophets among you, I, the Lord, would reveal myself in visions. I would speak to them in dreams. But not with my servant Moses. Of all my house, he is the one I trust. I speak to him face to face, clearly, and not in riddles! (Numbers 12:6-8)

God has chosen to speak to us in the riddles of our dreams instead of face to face like He did with Moses. God speaks to people throughout the Bible, but the way he speaks to them sometimes isn't mentioned. There are 113 occurrences in the Bible for the word 'dream' and 118 occurrences for the word 'vision' in the NLT translation. Both visions and dreams use symbols which the Holy Spirit leads us to meaning of. I don't think there is any difference between a vision or a dream but I don't hear about people having visions very often; however, we all have dreams at night. Therefore, my desire is to understand how God speaks to us through dreams. These are all the dreams I could find in the Bible:

Prophecy about about one's own life.

1. In Abram's dream God promised the land of Israel to his descendants and before that they would be enslaved for 400 years (see Genesis 15).

2. Joseph (son of Jacob) had a dream as a youth that his brothers bundles of grain bowed down to his, which meant he would reign over his brothers (see Genesis 37).

3. In Joseph's second dream the sun, moon, and eleven stars bowed before him—symbols of his mother and father and eleven brothers. (Later, the twelve brothers become the twelve tribes of Israel.) (see Genesis 37).

4. In Jacob's ladder or stairway dream God told Jacob He will give this land (Canaan) to his descendants and he will one day bring him back to this land (see Genesis 28:12).

5. A Midianite soldier had a dream of loaf a bread tumbling into their camp. It meant that Gideon would have victory over them (see Judges 7:13).

6. Solomon in his dream asked for wisdom and God gave him that, in addition to riches and fame (see 1 Kings 3).

There are also prophetic dreams about one's own life interpreted through someone with God's gift of dream interpretation. "God gave Daniel the special ability to interpret the meanings of visions and dreams" (Daniel 1:17). Joseph or Daniel were given the gift of interpretation of dreams—both of their own and others (i.e. Pharaoh and Nebuchadnezzar). This was before the Holy Spirit was given to us all. Now we can all hear from God the interpretation of our dreams—we look to the Holy Spirit to speak to our own hearts for the meaning of our dreams.

1. Joseph (son of Jacob) interpreted his jailmates' dreams. The cup-bearer and baker's dreams of three branches and baskets meant in three days one would be promoted by the Pharaoh and the other beheaded (see Genesis 40).

2. Joseph (son of Jacob) interpreted Pharaoh's dream of seven wheat shafts and cows as seven years of feast and famine (see Genesis 41).

3. Daniel interpreted Nebuchadnezzar's second dream of a large tree cut down and seven periods of time as symbolic of Nebuchadnezzar going insane for seven years (see Daniel 4).

God warns us.

1. God warned King Abimelech in a dream that he has been deceived and must give Abram his wife back or face destruction of his nation (see Genesis 20).

2. Laban (Jacob's father-in-law) is warned by God in a dream to not harm Jacob (see Genesis 31).

3. God warned the wise men (Magi) in a dream not to tell Herod where the baby Jesus was (see Matthew 2:12).

4. Pilate's wife had a nightmare that Jesus was innocent and told her husband to leave him alone (see Matthew 27:19).

God commands or guides us.

1. Twenty years later Jacob had a follow up to his earlier personal prophecy dream. He had a dream where God told him that He has blessed his flocks and to return to the land of Canaan (see Genesis 31).

2. God told Joseph (husband of Mary) to flee to Egypt from Herod in Bethlehem (see Matthew 2:13).

3. An angel told Joseph (husband of Mary) to go back to Israel (see Matthew 2:19).

God informs us.

1. God told Joseph (husband of Mary) that Mary was pregnant by the Holy Spirit with the son of God—who is to be named Jesus (see Matthew 1:20).

Gift of prophecy.

These are dreams that go beyond the normal limited scope of our lives, for example, to prophesy about whole countries, the world, and apocalyptic events (apocalyptic means symbolically predictive of future events). Even non-believers are given supernaturally prophetic dreams.

But there is a God in heaven who reveals secrets, and he has shown King Nebuchadnezzar what will happen in the future (Daniel 2:28).

1. Daniel interpreted King Nebuchadnezzar's dream of a gold, silver, bronze, and iron statue as symbolic of four kingdoms ruling the world before an everlasting kingdom (see Daniel 2).

2. Daniel dreamt of four animals that represent four kingdoms that come before the kingdom of Christ. God told Him that this dream is about events in the distant future (see Daniel 7).

3. In a dream Jeremiah is told of God restoring Israel after exile to Babylon (see Jeremiah 31:23-26).

Visions

It appears John's book of revelation wasn't a dream and came to him while he was exiled on the island of Patmos (for preaching the word of the Lord and for his testimony about Jesus). He was awake worshiping God in the Spirit and a loud voice spoke to him and he saw a vision (see Revelations 1:10). Ezekiel's apocalyptic prophecy was also a vision instead of a dream. Lastly, Zechariah had prophecies about the reconstruction of the temple. In Zechariah 4:1 he says and angel woke him as if he had been asleep. I don't know if this counts as a dream or not.

> *Dreams are messages from God but they are not the Word of God.*

Interpreting dreams is God's business (Genesis 40:8).

God wants you to understand what is in your heart and what is going to happen (paraphrase of Daniel 2:29-30). Is it possible that Nebuchadnezzar woke up disturbed by his dream but couldn't remember the dream and that is why he asked them to tell him what his dream was in addition to what it meant? We must look to the Holy Spirit not only for the meaning of a dream but for help in remembering a dream. Lastly, dreams are messages from God but they are not the Word of God. The Bible is the ultimate authority and messages from God will not contradict it. Read the whole Bible and spend more time studying it than you do your dreams.

Christian dream interpretation in the church.

"You cannot observe your dreams and remain a phony Christian for long. Dreams will reveal what you are doing and will not allow you to ignore it" (*Dream Interpretation: A Biblical Understanding* by Herman Riffel). God uses dreams to communicate with us. He guides us, warns us, and shows us the parts of our lives that we need to look at or surrender. Sometimes our dreams are God's way of bringing us to our knees through nightmares and yelling in our sleep. Riffel says that people in crisis (which include many defeated Christians) frequently are interested in understanding what God is trying to tell them through their dreams. Dreams are very rarely literal pictures foretelling events in other people's lives. Dreams are God's way of telling us about ourselves.

Many pastors (of many different denominations) are not open to the idea of dream interpretation because it takes a willingness to break out of the security of what they already have and know. Sometimes the business of being a church becomes more important than inner growth and many pastors have not experienced having to come to terms with their inner darkside or shadow.

Dreams rarely foretell events in other people's lives.

"Just because the churches have decided to pay no attention to their unconscious does not mean that God will stop trying to speak to us. So it is that scientific psychology and medicine, in search of a way to help us find healing and wholeness, have discovered what the Bible knew all along but Christians had forgotten: that dreams and their interpretation can heal the sick soul" (*Dreams: God's Forgotten Language*). Many churches reject psychology and Jung's theories. Psychology is a godless discipline and Jung wasn't a Christian but they have given us tools for understanding ourselves and our dreams. Of course, you don't have to know anything about psychology or Jung's theories for God to tell you the meaning of your dreams. However, if you learn more about how to interpret your dreams, it will be easier to understand more of God's messages.

"I think that dreams are especially needed by Charismatic and Pentecostal Christians who have found new power by an experience with the Holy Spirit" (*Dream Interpretation: A Biblical Understanding*). I belong to a Pentecostal church of the Foursquare denomination. I don't think we are closed-minded but we are focused church planting and to some degree the Holy Spirit (baptism of the Holy Spirit, speaking in tongues, laying on hands for spiritual healing, etc.) and lack an understanding of inner growth (and the corresponding discipleship). Why is the charismatic movement so into speaking tongues and so little is said about dreams? Part of the reason is the mis-conception that dreams are for prophecy about others, instead of a way to learn about ourselves through God. Riffel estimates only five percent of our dreams are actually about others. Christians go looking for literal prophecies about others in their dreams and when that doesn't work they lose confidence in dreams, but dreams are actually symbolic messages about ourselves. This confusion has been a tool of deception used by the enemy to keep us from listening to God's voice in our dreams.

One fellow church-member, who grew up Baptist, pointed out that Pentecostals shy away from intellectual understanding like Christian psychology. Dream interpretation does use some psychological concepts but shouldn't be lumped in with intellectual Christianity. The rational, intellectual approach to Christianity prevelant in so much of the Western culture is a huge deception in the church that makes so many people (like I once did) turn away and reject the church. Intellectual Christianity gives us debates on doctrine and esoteric interpretations of the Bible from ivory towers. We read one Christian book after another building up our knowledge but not growing spiritually. Intellectual Christianity cannot help the wounded seekers look inwards into the dark depths of our soul. Divinely empowered tools like spiritual-therapy (Solomon) and Christian dream interpretation (Riffel, Sanford, and Kelsey) must be used. Soul-transformation, and God using our dreams, pulls Christians out of the trenches of spiritual defeat and onto victorious lives.

"It is no wonder that intellectual theology is more popular in most Christian circles. Who wants to be wounded again and again—even if the new wounding brings new transformation and insight? Obviously, only a theology that understands the experience of human brokeness and hurt is able to help those who have been wounded and are seeking help."

"No one can be blamed for avoiding the individual, personal, religious encounter, except people who attempt to guide others, either personally or by writing religious and theological books. The average man or woman can find religious development within the church, where the divine encounter is transformed into lower voltage. They can slowly work at bringing their lives in line. This is not an inferior calling, just a different one..." (*Christo-Psychology*).

Shepherds of all forms (pastors, pastoral counselors, ministry leaders, small group leaders, etc.) in the church must be living victorious lives, otherwise, they are the defeated leading the defeated. Part of a victorious life is the Lord bringing our lives into balance (healing of unconscious conflicts, complexes, repressed parts of our personality, etc.) through the transformation provided by the Holy Spirit—which is can be done through listening to and working with our dreams.

Culture types, personality type, and Christian Dream interpretation.

Herman Riffel, who has traveled through 50 countries lecturing and presenting seminars on dreams, observed that western cultures aren't receptive to the idea of dream interpretation, whereas, the rest of the world is. On the other hand, the rest of the world is still learning about walking in the Holy Spirit.

"This quite different point of view, which finds dreams highly significant and meaningful, has been held in practically all other cultures. Indeed wherever, peoples have not been touched and influenced by our Western world-view with its belief that man is limited to sense experience and reason, the dream has been viewed as the chief medium through which non-physical (or spiritual) powers and realities spoke to man" (*DREAMS: The Dark Speech of the Spirit*).

I proved in my book, *Where in the World Do I Belong??*, that western culture is sensing and thinking—an STJ culture type. This is a concrete, realistic, rational and logical culture type which is the opposite of the subjective, intuitive nature of dreams. Western cultures may reject or resist listening to their dreams because they are sensing culture types. In Western cultures, intuition is a weak or inferior function and may be neglected or repressed (which becomes the shadow or darkside of the culture type). Western Christianity neglects the vital function dreams are to being a healthy Christian. In Western culture, dreams, like healing of the soul, have become prisoner to realm of psychology. They both belong in the church through spiritualtherapy and Christian dream interpretation facilitated by pastors, church elders, and shepherds.

According to the *MBTI Manual*, the American population is 26.7% intuitive personality types. Many intuitive personality types, like myself, are deeply

> **Many Christians are missing out on the incredible gift of dreams.**

interested in hearing from God through our dreams. My wife is a sensing personality type and doesn't have as much of an interest in dreams as I do; she looks more for the voice of God in her physical surroundings, or circumstances. We all have different personality types and God speaks to all us in a myriad of different ways, but some personality types might try to discount dreams and the inner growth possible through them. I highly admire and respect Joyce Meyer but even her wonderful book, *How to Hear From God*, gives us a good example of the misconception of dreams in mainstream Christianity: "Dreams are interesting but usually very unstable in giving us direction. People who try to make too much out of their dreams are asking to be deceived." Many Christians are missing out on the incredible gift of dreams. One person said that the uninterpreted dream is like an unopened letter. Are you reading your mail from God or treating it as spam?

Christian Dream interpretation.

Search the online version of the Bible (NLT) and there are 113 references to the word dream. Anyone who has read a little of the Bible can see that God uses dreams to speak to people. Herman Riffel, in his book *Dream Interpretation: A Biblical Understanding,* explains that a "dream is pointing up our problem, or solution, or perhaps direction, or challenge or correction." Riffel says dreams can be warnings or promises. If we heed the warning we won't face the consequences, and if we keep from evil ways we will reap the rewards of the promises. Pastor Mike Kai explained that God can call us to do something and if we ignore Him there are two things that can happen. He passes us over and gives the opportunity to someone else (and we are given another assignment) or He takes from us (sometimes painfully depending on how tight our grip is) the very thing that is keeping us from obeying His will. I have found that dreams are a very good place to hear God's warnings of the consequences of not obeying His will.

One atheist I know claims that he never has dreams. Since dreams are the voice of God, it's not surprising that God isn't talking to him because he isn't listening. Riffel warns people not to ignore the voice of God. "God might get their attention through pain by throwing them on a bed of suffering, So they can't stand the sight of food, have no appetite for their favorite treats. They lose weight, wasting away to nothing, reduced to a bag of bones. They hang on the cliff-edge of death, knowing the next breath may be their last" (Job 33:19-22). Boy, I've been there and done that, right before I surrendered my life to Christ and started going back to church.

Riffel tells us that, "No where in the Bible are we warned to be careful of dreams." However, Riffel found that some dreams can be from false sources. "As I spoke about dreams to a group of pastors in Singapore, some of them pointed out that their fathers had experienced dreams that told them not to listen to the missionaries. I was puzzled at first, but as we pointed out what God had said about those who go to idols, we soon recognized that this had happened because these older men had come from a corrupted Buddhist tradition; their dreams were influenced by these false sources."

Christian Dream interpretation and personality type.

"Jung made it his business to listen to dreams and other productions of the unconscious in a way that practically no other psychologist has attempted." Freud tried a rational approach to dreams but "Jung, on the contrary, suggested that the unconscious does not think rationally to begin with, but rather symbolically, metaphorically, in images" (*DREAMS: The Dark Speech of the Spirit*).

In our culture, symbolic thinking is a way of life for Christians but not for non-Christians. Jesus used symbols in his many parables and pastors constantly interpret the meaning of various symbols and metaphors in the Bible for their books and sermons.

There is no need to be a Jungian analyst, psychologist, or even pastor to be able to interpret your dreams. God made dreams into tools that any Christian (or non-Christian) can use to hear His voice. Some personality types have more interest in or are more adept at dream interpretation and translation, but anyone can learn to hear God's voice through their dreams.

C.G. Jung was an INTP, and INTPs have a gift for classifying and naming things for what they are. Many interpretations of dream symbols we use today are ones that Jung had defined. My personality type is INFP, and INFPs have a gift for interpreting symbols and metaphors—which is what dream interpretation is all about. I also have the spiritual gift of wisdom which is useful in determining how a dream symbol relates to mine or another persons spiritual life and real (conscious/ awake) life.

There is no need to be a Jungian analyst, psychologist, or even pastor to be able to interpret your dreams.

The important part of interpretation is not to take these symbols as literal translations but find definitions of the symbol that resonates with what's going on in your life. I like to use this website to quickly find dream symbol meanings: http://en.mimi.hu/dreams/index_dreams.html

There are several meanings that can be attached to any dream symbol. For example, in a recent dream I was wearing a red tuxedo.

The color red can mean:

1. Great passion and sensitivity in your emotional relationships.

2. Sacrifice and sex.

3. Danger, proceed with caution around the thing that is red.

4. The color of anger, which could be a warning to stay cool and keep your temper under control.

Basically red is about passion, sexuality, danger, anger, or warning. In my case I looked at the surrounding symbols in my dream and what was going on in my life and realized it was a warning message from God that in my anger I wouldn't see things clearly. And sure enough there was a situation in my life that day that my anger could have really made things worse. The actual message of the dream was much more complex than this, but the basic message was a warning about my anger in an upcoming situation.

Christian Dream interpretation and personality type part II

We can look at dreams from the standpoint of your Myers Briggs personality type. I am a strong intuitive type and find that I pay attention to signs from God in dreams more than in the physical world. My wife, other the other hand, being a strong sensing type, notices signs from God everywhere and sometimes isn't as interested in dream interpretations as I am. Recently, my wife is seeing many signs with the message of the water of life.

Jesus said, "Everyone who drinks this water will get thirsty again and again. Anyone who drinks the water I give will never thirst—not ever. The water I give will be an artesian spring within, gushing fountains of endless life." (John 4:13)

This was mentioned in two different DVD series that we were watching. Then the message was on a balloon our son brought back from sunday school had the words "Jesus is living water—eternally refreshing." There was also a sermon on the water of life in her Japanese language Bible study (from a missionary from Japan). And recently she had a dream about going to a new frozen yogurt shop and finding out it hadn't opened for business yet. There was no dream definition for frozen yogurt but ice cream is a symbol for satisfaction. We heard another sermon on living water at our church about finding satisfaction in the Lord and not in other things. We can go around in life searching for things that fulfill us, but if we drink of his living water (His life, Word and Holy Spirit) we will never be thirsty again.

Dreams and the Holy Spirit transformation.

A dream comes when there are many cares (Eccl. 5:3).

Many people who are interested in dream interpretation may be in crisis or have experienced a crisis (financial, marital, addiction, abuse, death, etc.). Some people may have been brought to their end (and as a result surrendered to God) through, among other things, consistent nightmares. Before I surrendered I occasionally had dreams that would cause me to scream at night. Why? Because God was trying to reach me; trying to show me the inbalance in my life; the repressed parts of myself; the twisted behaviors that came out of my inner vows; the prison I had place myself in through bitterness and lack of forgiveness; the intellectual idols I worshipped like passion and calling; but most of all the need to die to myself and be resurrected in my new identity in Christ. Other people may be experiencing a time of change in there lives. Bruce Saunders came to know Riffel (author of *Dream Interpretation: A Biblical Understanding*) and his teachings "at the perfect time for my personal growth—just before a time of great personal and professional upheaval. Working through dreams that accompany a season of change and growth was incredibly valuable to me, and has been to others I know as well" (*An Overview of Dream interpretation*).

Dreams are the voice of God and an important tool the Holy Spirit uses for transformation, healing and wholeness. However, we can't experience this healing without dying to ourselves first. Then we must be willing to face our inner shadow—the unconscious immature parts (emotional, mental, spiritual) of our personality. Once we are surrendered, God takes us up on our offering our lives and begins to transform our mind and emotions (although this might not be right away—it's all according to God's timing).

Many people want to learn how to prophesy and interpret other people's dreams. What they don't understand is that dreams are about the dreamer—and the dreamer is the best person to interpret them. As we learn how to interpret our own dreams we understand what God wants to show us about ourselves. The methods of dream interpretation are easy to learn. Bruce Saunders pointed out that people already use analogy and simile in everyday situations and symbolic dream interpretation is the same thing.

Understanding our dreams takes a willingness to grow, be healed and made whole. Understanding your unconscious side can bring harmony, freedom, passion, and vitality. God wants to show us our unconscious complexes (inner conflicts and repressed parts of ourselves) so that we can surrender them to Him and be healed and balanced. He does the searching for us and shows us our blindspots through our dreams, but sometimes we can be so blind to our blindspots that even in interpreting our dreams we can miss the point or message. Sometimes we need to bounce the dream off of someone who knows us really well. My spouse is a very different personality type from mine and consistently sees things in waking life that I don't notice and vice versa. The same goes for our unconscious lives, we can see each others blind spots that are being communicated in the other's dream.

Herman Riffel points out one indicator that we are making progress:

"Weddings are exciting, and when they occur in a dream they often speak of a great union. Since a dream is seeking to bring us into wholeness, it always desires the integration of the various aspects of our inner life. The shadow figures, which are hidden in the darkness of our hearts, are usually brought into consciousness first and yielded to God for correction and growth. Then the masculine and feminine traits may be brought into conscious balance. This may take months or even years."

"There comes a time when the person begins to dream of preparing for a wedding. It is the wedding of the shadow figure with the masculine or feminine aspect. It is a sign of wholeness. That does not mean, of course, that no more growth is necessary, but it does indicate that an integration of the personality is taking place" (*Dream Interpretation: A Biblical Understanding*).

Eventually, we become whole and our lives are brought in line with God's will, and then, as a result, we experience more of God's intended supernatural blessings in our lives.

Christian dream interpretation, masculine, feminine, and Myers Briggs personality types.

Dreams are almost always about ourselves. The people and places in our dreams represent something in ourselves. Even the recognizable people we see in our dreams are just representations of our feelings about those people applied to ourselves. In other words, we might have a dream of our old boss who was a tyrant, but the dream is really about how we are acting, or something we are repressing in our waking life. Places in our dreams are personifications of ourselves. In other words, a house or car may represent our body, mind and personality, conscious life or ego. Different rooms represent different aspects of ourselves, the basement is our unconscious, the kitchen portray how we nourish ourselves and others, the bathroom is where we relieve or cleanse ourselves of emotional waste. The living room is like a car in a dream and can represent our persona—the person we show to others, the way we portray ourselves to others.

Sometimes we project onto others. Projecting means that we take the negative qualities (sometimes unconscious) in ourselves and see them as problems in others or something we fear. For example, if someone bothers me because I feel they have an over-confidence in their gifts and abilities, this is really a call to myself to have more confidence in myself and my own gifts and abilities. Dreams are a mirror pointing to ourselves and many times the part of ourselves that we ignore and project upon others. For instance, if I think someone is a controlling person in real (conscious/waking) life, then my dreams might show me that I am frustrated with my inability to take control of my life. If I listen and act on that need for correction (learned from my dream) that person no longer bothers me.

There are a few symbols that are frequent in our dreams, one of which is our shadow or darkside. Things we project on others are examples of our shadow and usually show up in our dreams. The shadow isn't evil, it's basically the immature or undeveloped parts (emotionally, mentally, spiritually) of our lives. The other common symbols are our masculine and feminine sides, which correlate with thinking and feeling personality type preferences or traits (see my book *Where in the World Do I Belong??*). For a man, in a dream, his feminine side might show up as, "mother, then as sweetheart, as the image or the soul, as seductress, as witch, as spiritual guide, as a little child, as a divine woman" (*Dreams: God's Forgotten Language*). Dreams of having sex with some anonymous person is actually just a representation of either our masculine or feminine sides. It is a symbol of deep connection with that part of ourselves.

There is a close correlation between masculine and feminine behaviors, and thinking and feeling personality types. As an introverted feeling personality type, I had some high ideals that led to me repressing some masculine parts of myself because I didn't want to be an aggressive, competitive, greedy, self-centered, egotistical male. A large part of this was a reaction to feeling marginalized in American culture which rewards thinking type behaviors—especially in men. Christianity supports many of the values that are central to my feeling personality type. Christians are taught to serve others which is a feeling type trait; on the other hand, American culture supports an objective thinking approach where everyone is responsible for their own welfare.

As a result of repressing my masculine side, I had also thrown out the good qualities of masculinity: protection of self and family; self-esteem; confidence in myself and my accomplishments; and taking control of my life. My dreams pointed to my problem for a long time, but I didn't understand until recently when I started to interpret my dreams. I had dreams about fights with male family members. These dreams were warnings to not repress my masculine side, as well as, my extroverted-thinking, which is my inferior function. It was the Lord, all along, trying to tell me what my problem was. As soon as I understood, I broke this inner vow (to not be like the stereotypical masculine, thinking male) and submitted this area of my life to the Lord. As a result, I was freed from the bondage of that vow and develop a healthy balance between my masculine and feminine, and thinking and feeling sides.

Christian dream interpretation, prophecy, and faith.

I have always believed my dreams have something to say but it wasn't until I read Riffel's book last year that I understood that dreams were God telling me something about myself. For the last year I have been journaling my dreams and God has been using them to guide me in my inner growth. As Joyce Meyer puts it: God really is more concerned with changing us rather than our circumstances.

Riffel explained that our dreams are more a diagnosis instead of a prophecy. They tell us where our actions are leading us and thus give us fair warning for correction but never condemnation. I usually have dreams giving me guidance and revealing my inner stumbling blocks, but I've also had some dreams that are prophetic (not about others but for myself). They show me partly symbolic and partly literal something that happens that day or week. This could be also categorized as a diagnosis dream but I don't make the connection until after it's already happened so I don't think it fits as a diagnosis. This is one area I am exploring.

The spiritual gift of prophecy is God using us to communicate a message that needs to be said and heard. The spiritual gift of prophecy isn't about revealing the future but instead gives us God's perspective on our current reality—also in a sort of diagnosis way: repent or make a correction or suffer the natural consequences (but not punishment from

God because those who believe in Christ are freed from condemnation).

God has been showing me more on prophecy lately through the books of Jeremiah, Daniel, and Ezekiel. Jeremiah's gift of prophecy is pretty straightforward: God tells him what the Israelites badly need to hear about their wicked ways and Jeremiah conveys it to the people of Israel but they refuse to listen. Ezekiel's visions are intense and puzzling. The book of Daniel includes more dreams. I can easily see the connection between Daniel's interpretations and the symbols in his dreams.

One friend heard I was reading Daniel and gave me a book on preterism, a doctrine stating the Bibles prophecies have already been fulfilled. For example, Daniel (7:7-14, 17, 18, 26, 27 also 2:44) had a dream of four kingdoms that would pass before the Messiah's Kingdom. The preterist interpretation of this prophecy is that the last kingdom represents the Roman empire's destruction of Jerusalem and the temple in 70 A.D. and that Jesus reigned as King after that.

Jesus kept telling people that some of them would live to see His kingdom come, and He said the current generation would not pass before He came into His reign. I believe that after his death on the cross He was crowned King in heaven and was resurrected here on earth, and from that time on began the spiritual reign of His kingdom on earth. However, I don't know if I believe that Daniel's prophecy was about the Roman empire or not.

The preterist or postmillenial doctrine is one possible way to interpret the prophecies of the Bible. This doctrine is extensive and what I have read of it certainly is thought provoking, but it's hard for me to judge it as Biblical or not.

J.F. Foster, an Amazon reviewer, commented on preterism: "If the Christian church has been dead wrong for the last 2,000 years about the central event in the consumation of all history, what kind of doctrine of the church are we left with? If the church has been wrong for its entire history on this question, what are we to say of the ability of the Holy Spirit to preserve his church and lead it in truth and righteousness?" I believe in the omnipotent power of the Holy Spirit so his argument may be enough to refute this unorthodox interpretation of prophecies in the the Bible. In all honesty, I'm still learning and praying that the Holy Spirit guide me to the truth.

Don't get caught up in debates about end-times prophecy instead focus on loving God and others.

So you might be wondering what exactly God is showing me in my dreams? Here is a recent one. There is more to the dream but this is the core part:

It's evening and four people (that I know very well except for one) are getting ready to have adulterous affairs upstairs (in my house) by sneaking in the windows. I've had enough of this activity and shine the light on their activities by letting others know and the authorities/police arrive. They all shuffle out of the house.

After waking up, I lay quiet in my bed and listened for the Holy Spirit to speak to my inner conscious. He surprisingly showed me what it meant. I realize that (to me) adultery ultimately means self destruction, and each of the people in my dream represent a facet of that in me. One person I know lacks faith (in my perception) and thus in my dream symbolically represents my lack of faith, the second person my inner Pharisee (loving God but not others). The third and fourth person seemed to represent dishonesty, but my feelings (or lingering bitterness) were getting in the way (just like your head (or thinking mind) can get in the way when you interpret dreams). The Lord moved me to look at an aloha card (from a sermon) in my wallet and showed me the words I was looking for. I thought they represented dishonesty and lack of integrity but looking deeper they really symbolize (in my life) a lack of commitment and irresponsibility.

The most emotional part of the dream (which is a sign from God that this is an important message in the dream) was with the commitment person. God's message to me is to be committed first off, and then responsible and loving (instead of a Pharisee).

I've also been reading Jeremiah and Ezekiel and God uses the word adulterous many times to describe the Israelites that are worshipping false Gods. My dream isn't about my worship of other things instead of God, but is really is an overall message of a lack of faith in Him that has dropped to the level of an unbeliever. The most important message of the dream was this message of lack of faith because it was repeated four times in my dream. God is telling me to have complete faith in Him—especially since He gave me such a huge gift of faith—the kind of faith that keeps me open instead of protective, loving instead of neutral, humble instead of proud, trusting instead of self empowering.

Because dreams are from God they have a supernatural quality. There are meanings on so many levels that apply both to our inner lives and the reality around us. I am familiar with three of the people in the dream but the fourth I know only on a superficial level. This is the one that represents my lack of faith. God has given me such a huge gift of faith that it's rare that I don't have it, so that is why a lack of faith is symbolized by a person I don't know very well. The other three people I am very close to and know very well and thus represent very real challenges for me: the need to be committed, responsible, and loving.

Preterism, dream interpretation, and faith.

The doctrine of preterism is the belief that the prophecies in the Bible (regarding end times and last days) were fulfilled in the first century after Christ's birth. Whether you believe the prophecy in the Bible (Daniel & Revelations) has already happened or not, this has no bearing on what God has called us to do. We are to live victorious lives by letting Christ live His life through us, and to love God and others.

One thing we can be sure of is that the prophecy in the Bible is an example of how God speaks both literally and symbolically to us through our dreams. Daniel tells us his dreams and then tells us the interpretation that the Holy Spirit has spoken to his heart. This is a clear example of what we are to do in our own lives. There are also the dreams of Jeremiah that speak literally instead of symbolically. For example, this is what Jeremiah heard in a dream before waking up:

This is what the Lord of Heaven's Armies, the God of Israel, says: "When I bring them back from captivity, the people of Judah and its towns will again say, 'The Lord bless you, O righteous home, O holy mountain!' Townspeople and farmers and shepherds alike will live together in peace and happiness. For I have given rest to the weary and joy to the sorrowing." At this, I woke up and looked around. My sleep had been very sweet. (Jeremiah 31:23-26)

Lastly, God can speak His desires through everyone's dreams—not just to people with the gift of prophecy. For example, you don't need the spiritual gift of faith to have faith in God. It's just that people who the spiritual gift of faith will be given (by the Holy Spirit) a supernatural gifting of faith—something not possible through that persons own capabilities. A spiritual gift of faith is a supernatural confidence and belief in God moving in situations that are impossible (for man). People with this gift are drawn to stepping out in faith in impossible situations like David did with Goliath. Pastor Mike Kai pointed out that when faith steps in, fear steps out and that God also used that "Hebrew hick-boy", David, to inspire unreal faith in others. Daniel, Jeremiah and Ezekiel had the spiritual gift of prophecy and God used their dreams in 'unreal' (supernaturally empowered) ways. Their dreams spoke God's truth to the people of many countries (Israel, Babylon, Assyria, Egypt, etc.).

6

Hope Chapel: Pentecostal with a passion for planting

I am a member of Hope Chapel and as part of my self-discipleship I felt called to understand our church better. Our church is part of the International Church of the Foursquare Gospel denomination. We are Pentecostal churches with a calling to planting new churches.

Hope Chapel Hawaii and the spirit-driven life.

Pastor Moore is an expert on church planting and Senior Pastor of Hope Chapel Kaneohe Bay. I am a member of Hope Chapel West Oahu, which is a church led by, Pastor Mike Kai, a former youth pastor and disciple of Moore.

I have to admire the theme in Pastor Moore's book, *Let Go of the Ring* (1993, 2000), of continual surrender to Christ's calling and God's will for his life. This is my biggest attraction to Hope Chapel: the example of authentic Christian living through giving complete control and Lordship of our lives to Christ. Moore believes, "The Bible is very consistent. God forces everyone He blesses to relinquish the ring of power before He does His part."

We also have to be careful of pride and impatience, Pastor Moore states, "It's easy to get ahead of God. You start with a sense of calling, add some legitimate success, toss in a new vision and you become pretty self important." "Pride leads to destruction, even if it is wrapped in spirituality and a sense of mission." "All those Bible heroes suffered loss of face before inheriting God's success."

"His plans work because they include unseen elements that we could never understand or anticipate." Moore quotes Schuller, "If there is something you think God has called you to do and if there is any way you can envision accomplishing it, then it probably wasn't God calling. Because God will only call you to do things that are bigger than you are, something bigger than your personal resources."

I like Pastor Moore's idea to use MiniChurch as a discussion laboratory of how we are applying to our lives the scripture taught the previous Sunday. "We examine our lives for authentic Christianity in the discussions we share in MiniChurch." One benefit of MiniChurch is that pastors don't get burned out because: "The pastoral counseling load is vastly reduced as people share each other's burdens (Galatians 6:2)." My only concern is that pastoral counseling should still be offered by churches.

In his recent sermon on TV (1-21-08) Moore reports that Hillsong Church in Australia has only 30% of church members involved in MiniChurches or small groups and his church Hope Chapel Kaneohe Bay has 60%. Wikipedia claims Hillsong is the largest Pentecostal church with a membership exceeding 19,000. Our church, Hope Chapel West Oahu, has about 850 members and thirty MiniChurches. If each MiniChurch averages ten people, that's about three hundred total in MiniChurch, which equals about 35% of our congregation.

Moore's calling is to evangelize, equip and reproduce. "We all come to the church as if it were a hospital for the spiritually sick. In time, we should grow beyond patient status and become members of the healing team." "If our church exists to equip God's people to do his work, we must ask, 'What is his work?' His work involves evangelism and church-planting. Individual Christians are called to reproduce themselves."

One blog mentioned Rick Warren's book, and how we are to submit to God's vision and ride the wave He is creating, instead creating our own wave or vision. In his recent sermon, Pastor Moore recommends Rick Warrens book, A *Purpose Driven Life*, but he said we must go a step beyond and develop a Spirit-driven life.

Gen-Xers coming to the cross and Christ.

Gen-Xers, like myself, are about ten years later than Boomers in starting a family and coming to the church. My mother was born-again in Christ at age 28 and I finally experienced the cross at age 38. She also had kids ten years early than I did. You tend to come to Christ in hard times and raising a family is very difficult. Gen-Xers are marrying and having kids later than Boomers; therefore, are coming to the church and being reborn at a later age. But reaching Gen-Xers takes much more than changing music styles of worship.

In his book, *Friends: The Key to Reaching Generation X* (1997, 2001), Pastor Moore, of Hope Chapel Kaneohe Bay in Hawaii, teaches Boomer's how to cross-culturally

communicate the truth of God to Gen-Xers. Moore classifies
Generation X as the years 1961-1981.

I have a lot of cross-cultural experience, and have
written a couple books about culture shock and culture
differences, so I liked this book. Living in Hawaii we learn
to communicate cross-culturally and Moore takes this a step
further by teaching the truth of Christ cross-generationally.
Even though this book was written eleven years ago, based
on a recent mainland church experience, he is still ahead of
the curve in cross-generational understanding in the church.
I wish I would have read this eleven years ago when it was first
published!

Moore addresses the barriers that kept me, and many of
my generation, from seeing the truth in Christ:

"Gen-Xers have gone through so much 'hell,' personally
or vicariously, that they are not scared by the real thing."
"Gen-Xers have much to forgive. This is the most neglected,
abused and sexually assaulted group on the American scene.
They struggle with moral debt more than the financial sins
of their parents." Gen-Xers are "more interested in enduring
relationships and hunger for intimacy to replace broken
families." "Gen-Xers respond well to a heavenly Dad who
offers unconditional love." We like this idea because he will
never fail us, always be our security, emotional and spiritual
support. I believe we also have a greater need for pastoral
counseling than other generations.

"An intellectual approach to a distant, dusty God does
nothing to solve the AIDS crisis or feed starving children.
Gen-Xers cannot be satisfied unless love and feeling enter
the salvation portrait. This feeling must result in Christians
producing answers to the pain Gen-Xers see all around. They

want to witness the reality of the second great commandment: Love your neighbor as yourself."

I absolutely agree with Moore that we Gen-Xers strive for authenticity, and experience it through personal testimony, authentic leaders, mentoring/discipling, experiencing the Holy Spirit, and miracles fulfilled from prayer—these are keys to our conversion! Moore has captured the Gen-Xer Starbucks mentality (or need) through small MiniChurch groups. "Generation X values intimacy over a crowd. This suggests that Gen-Xers may never build megachurches."

While on vacation back in Colorado I had the opportunity to attend services at the biggest churches in Fort Collins and Windsor. They had large video screens, Boomer pastors, and concert-like worship. However, technology doesn't impress me. I like to hear my own voice during worship, and I prefer a small congregation—which feels more like family.

"Gen-Xers compensate for elevated expectations with blinding loyalty, especially in the church." I love Moore's concepts of mentoring, disciplining, and hiring within; depending on "Holy Spirit-anointed leadership" instead of relying on Seminary credentials. "The first step to risk taking when appointing leadership is to trust that the Lord will reveal the right people through supernatural as well as natural means." "Today nearly 60 percent of Foursquare pastors entered the professional ministry without a formal theological degree." The pastor of my church, Hope Chapel West Oahu, is a product of Moore's leadership development system.

Truly, one of the many factors of my coming to back to Christ, was having a Gen-X pastor who spoke to me in my language, despite me being a white, mainlander and him being a Big Island, Filipino. I agree with Moore that The New Living Translation "has opened the door to personal Bible reading for the first time in their lives." Last year, I received an NLT Bible from Pastor Mike when I rededicated my life to Christ. I was amazed how much I enjoyed reading the NLT Bible. The old feelings of the Bible being inaccessible and irrelevant fell away.

"Building to Jesus involves crucifixion. When I was young, I died to my planned career in architecture. The cross of my life was a call to ministry. I envisioned a life of sure misery, but I said yes. The rewards have been significant." When Moore first came to Hawaii he spent all his money on trying to plant a new church and thought he would have to leave the ministry and get job selling cars or something, but then God started the blessings.

The message of the cross escapes many Christians. This message is extremely important for Gen-Xers like myself. Moore states throughout his book, Gen-Xers crave authenticity. The message of the cross and the resulting victory in Christ is as authentic as it gets. I believe experiencing the cross and a new identity in Christ is key to reaching my generation.

Pastoral Care, MiniChurch, and the Cross

Pastor Moore's church planting philosophy, in his book *Starting a New Church*, is equipping and training many leaders within the church that may eventually go on to plant new churches. During a speech at Hope Chapel Central in 2008, he said there are now 700 daughter churches of Hope Chapel.

This rapid growth process with leadership born in the trenches reminds me of the Silicon Valley tech startups.

The first year I worked in Silicon Valley I did a year of self studies on and off the job, passed eight different test and became a certified systems engineer. Because of rapid growth and incredible demand, I was hired for positions I didn't have experience for and learned on-the-fly or on-the-job. A self-disciple approach might be necessary in this new rapid church growth model, where discipleship and pastoral care may be considered a luxury.

When considering a place to hold church services, Moore even points out that companies like HP and Amazon were started in garages. "Maintain the camping aura of ministry and your people will be less demanding of the service aspects of ministry and more willing to contribute time and energy to providing those services" (*Starting a New Church*). Once again this resonates with my Silicon Valley experience, as a technical support person, I was better off doing my own research and troubleshooting than calling outside customer support for software problems. Customer support lines were impossible to get through, and the reps didn't know any more than I did.

Pastor Moore's philosophy is: "Rather than care for the saints, we are called to train them to serve others" (*Starting a New Church*). I believe, we must care for the saints who have not experienced the cross before we train them to serve; otherwise, they will be serving out of the flesh and self-effort instead of a God centered and spirit-controlled life.

Salvation deals with our sins but the cross deals with the power of sin over our lives. The cross is the death of our self centered, self-controlled life to a resurrection into the life of Christ through complete submission, commitment, and surrender to control of our lives by the Holy Spirit.

"The unbeliever is convicted of sin; the believer must be convicted of self if he is to see the need for it to be dealt with by the cross" (*The Ins and Outs of Rejection*). There are no half measures. God requires that we give our complete life to him; then we experience the spiritual transformation and renewal of our minds, and the subsequent joy, peace, and blessings of victory in Christ.

What is victory like? "There may be instantaneous deliverance from some defeating attitudes and behavior while others are not even touched or brought to conscious awareness. This is parallel to sins in a person's life at conversion. Some drop away immediately while others are pointed out by the Holy Spirit at a later stage in the growth process" (*The Ins and Outs of Rejection*).

"There is much more emphasis placed on evangelism than on discipleship by a great preponderance of churches. Since this is the case, many believers live their entire lives without even knowing that appropriation of the victorious life is a live option." (*The Ins and Outs of Rejection*).

It is vital that pastors through pastoral care convey the message of the cross. "Luke 14:27 states we are not disciples unless we have taken up the cross" (*The Ins and Outs of Rejection*). At Hope Chapel, members are discipled by shepherds (small group leaders) of MiniChurches. Moore considers MiniChurches the "on-the-job training center for a new generation of pastoral leadership" (*Let Go of the Ring*). Therefore, shepherds of MiniChurches must be equipped and trained to share the message of the cross.

Bottom line: we must teach the message of the cross before we train saints to serve or they will experience the self defeat of struggling to do the will of God using their own will-power and self effort. If we train them to serve before leading them to victory they will eventually experience defeat. I have no problem with the transfer of some pastoral care to ministry leaders and MiniChurch shepherds, as long as you send out these mini-apostles trained to disciple their flock in the message of the cross.

Building wealth as a Christian

At Hope Central, Pastor Moore, of Hope Chapel Kaneohe Bay, spoke at a Life After Debt seminar. He explained that many of us Christians have a 'poverty is humility' mentality that isn't right. God wants us to prosper and to use our wealth to bless others. He recommended many secular publications, such as Kiplingers and Money magazine, for learning how to grow wealth.

I bought Moore's book, *Your Money*, to better understand how to grow wealth in a Christian way. Moore quotes John Wesley, the early leader of the Methodist movement, "Get all you can, save all you can, and give all you can."

We live in a fallen world and even though we are not of it, we still have to make a living in it and save for the future (kid's college, retirement, etc). We have to use the means available to us that we feel led by God to use. We will be held accountable for how we use the gifts that the Lord has given us. We shouldn't reject the blessings, gifts or opportunities the Lord gives us, but I still wonder where to draw the line. For example, if I invest in real estate for profit doesn't that raise prices and hurt families (especially here in Hawaii)?

The first place to start is tithing. God will bless you abundantly when you tithe: "Bring the whole tithe into the storehouse, that there may be food in my house. Test me in this," says the LORD Almighty, "and see if I will not throw open the floodgates of heaven and pour out so much blessing that there will not be room enough to store it" (Mal 3:10). This verse reminds me of a t-shirt my brother had as a kid that said "Try it You'll like it!"

Moore in his book, *Your Money*, explained, "God enlarged upon his message through Malachi by saying, 'Try it! Let me prove it to you!' God wanted the people to put Him to the test, to prove whether the promise proved true. This is the only place in the Bible where God invites us to test Him. So if your not tithing now, why not try it?" Moore is confident that, "At the end of six months you will want to continue tithing." "It's easy to know where to tithe: it is where we're spiritually fed, week in and out."

7

Christians are called to Justice

There are endless forms of injustice in society but God has burdened me with the injustice of economic inequality. God has given me a burden not for charity but for justice and Nicholas Wolterstorff in his essay *Justice, Not Charity* clarifies exactly what this means. (I haven't read it but Wolterstorff goes even deeper into the meaning of justice in his book called *Justice*.) The spiritual gift of wisdom is the ability to apply Biblical principles to real life situations, and Wolterstorff, through his gift of wisdom, articulates God's truth of our Christian (and non-Christian) responsibility for justice along with charity. We should not use one to excuse the other. We must seek justice for the downtrodden and misfortunate. We are called not only to do acts of charity but also to work to remove the injustice that caused them to need charity.

Is this not the fast that I choose:
to loose the bonds of injustice,
to undo the thongs of the yoke,
to let the oppressed go free,
and to break every yoke?

Is it not to share your bread with the hungry,
and bring the homeless poor into your house;
when you see the naked, to cover them,
and not to hide yourself from your own kin?
(Isaiah 58:6-7).
The Spirit of the Lord God is upon me,
because the Lord has anointed me:
he has sent me to bring good news to the oppressed,
to bind up the brokenhearted,
to proclaim liberty to the captives,
and release to the prisoners;
(Isaiah 61:1).

> *Charity doesn't let Christians off the hook of fighting injustice.*

"The passage in Isaiah which Jesus read or referred to spoke not only of sharing one's bread with the hungry, bringing the homeless poor into one's house, and clothing the naked, but also of loosing the bonds of injustice, undoing the thongs of the yoke, letting the oppressed go free, and breaking every yoke. One not only tends to the victims of injustice but looses the bonds that make them victims" (*Justice, Not Charity*).

Christians must understand that charity doesn't let them off the hook of fighting injustice. "Rendering justice to the victims of injustice requires going beyond aiding victims; it requires attacking the victimizers—be they individual persons, social organizations and institutions, or whatever." "Christians should not only alleviate the distress of the downtrodden, but become their advocates against those who oppress them" (*Justice, Not Charity*).

So where does God fit in Social Justice?

Justice for me is about applying universal truths (from God) to real life situations. Social Justice is about getting together various groups that are all working towards some piece of universal truth. I suppose we all believe our own personal tuning into universal truth is the best avenue for social change. I personally believe that equality (social, economic, and recognizing and rewarding individuals, etc.) is the master key that will bring about a lot of other universal truths (clean environment, end of violence, etc.).

The most successful social change movement has a spiritual base. Social change occurs by God's grace, his divine supernatural power, moving within each individual and society and spiritually transforming everyone. "Great men... all left their mark on Earth, precisely because their minds were occupied with Heaven...we shall never save civilisation as long as civilisation is our main object" (*Mere Christianity* by C.S. Lewis).

What's important to social change is not a self-empowered movement but a spiritual empowerment by God. The closest thing to an embodiment of God's supernatural power is the church. There certainly aren't any super-heroes in the church but the power that flows through the body of the church is super-powered by God's grace and Holy Spirit. Philip Yancey writes, "For all its flaws the church at times has, fitfully and imperfectly to be sure, dispensed Jesus' message of grace to the world. It was Christianity, and only Christianity, that brought the end to slavery, and Christianity that inspired the first hospitals and hospices to treat the sick. The same energy drove the early labor movement, women's suffrage, prohibition, human rights campaigns, and civil rights" (*What's so Amazing About Grace*).

The Salvation Army was also started as a Christian mission. "They feed the hungry, shelter the homeless, treat addicts and alcoholics, and show up first at disaster scenes. The movement has continued to grow so that today these soldiers of grace number a million—one of the world's largest standing armies—and serve in a hundred countries" (*What's so Amazing About Grace*).

Christian character is what is needed for movements like the environment. "Our culture says, 'If you don't own it, you won't take care of it.' But Christians live by a higher standard: Because God owns it, I must take the best care of it that I can" (*The Purpose Driven Life*).

I've got a particular calling towards righting the inequality in society, however C.S. Lewis explains my conundrum: "There is a paradox about tribulation in Christianity. Blessed are the poor, but by 'judgment' (i.e. Social Justice) and alms we are to remove poverty wherever possible" (*The Problem of Pain*). The poor have more of a reason to be dependent on God and as a result it is easier for them to receive God's grace and blessings. I feel a calling to right the injustice of inequality in the U.S. and the world but by doing so am I giving people less of a reason to turn to God?

Is social change more effective through changing lives instead of changing laws? Yancey points out how unpolitical Jesus was. "Jesus' images portray the kingdom as a kind of secret force. Sheep among wolves, treasure hidden in a field, the tiniest seed in the garden, wheat growing among weeds, a pinch of yeast worked into bread dough, a sprinkling of salt on meat—all these hint at a movement that works within society, changing it from the inside out" (*What's so Amazing About Grace*). Yancey gives the fall of the Roman Empire and the crumbling of Communism as evidence that Christianity is more powerful and lasting than any national power or political movement. Should we concentrate our social change on people (and as result society) instead of laws?

Christianity is not "salvation from this earthly existence, but a religion of salvation from injustice in this earthly existence". Matthew 25:31-46 "is about justice. It says that to alleviate the condition of the social least is to render them what justice requires. It is not to go beyond justice into the realm of charity and benevolence; it is to render to them what justice requires. To fail to come to their aid is not simply to fail in charity or to be less than fully righteous. It is to wrong them. And the passage gives a truly awesome significance to wronging them: to wrong the social least is, whether one realizes it or not, to wrong Jesus Christ himself" (*Justice, Not Charity: Social Work through the Eyes of Faith* by Nicholas Wolterstorff).

8

Culture and Faith

Great Men of Faith

I had the honor and pleasure to meet, Neil Verwey, an 85 year old Christian missionary and founder of Japan Mission. His sermon was in Japanese, and I only understood about a third of it, so I felt it necessary to buy his autobiography: *Half a Century in Japan.*

In his autobiography he mentioned Hudson Taylor, a famous missionary to China in 1855, as an inspiration for acts of great faith. The next day after finishing Verwey's book I put it away in my bookshelf leaving it up to God if He wanted to show me more on this subject. The very next day, by an act of grace, I stumbled on Taylor's autobiography (and I wasn't in a bookstore or library). Is God trying to tell me something? I guess I'm attracted to these men and their stories because they have the same spiritual gifts of apostleship and faith that I do.

Recently, I prayed for understanding, wisdom, and faith in relying on God to provide for our needs—to give Him complete and total control and responsibility for all our needs (financial, etc). In both books, I was amazed at the reliance on God for finances. Verwey took many leaps of faith, like signing year contracts for radio and newspaper evangelism projects before God had provided the money. One time someone made a donation to the mission just in the nick of time, another time someone in the office opened a package and cash fell out onto the floor.

Taylor started out by learning to rely on God for food and rent money. After much resistance, God convicted Taylor to give his last coin to a homeless family, and immediately he felt a rush of joy and peace from the Holy Spirit. "He who giveth to the poor lendeth to the Lord: I asked Him not to let my loan be a long one," said Hudson. The next day an anonymous person sent him money (four times the amount) in the mail. Taylor proclaimed, "How glad the merchants of Hull would be if they could lend their money at such a rate! I then and there determined that a bank which could not break should have my savings or earnings as the case might be—a determination I have not yet learned to regret." I love Taylor's idea that God is the best bank for our money.

Christianity in Japan and Culture Types

Several people have said that the Christian movement in Japan is beginning to take off. In our conversation, Neil Verwey said that ever since 1963 the number of conversions has dropped off. The Japanese obsession with materialism has been biggest obstacle to conversion to Christianity in Japan. He said some of the youth are being reached through music, but the harvest in Japan is more like a fruit orchard, where every piece of fruit must be picked individually and handled carefully. Is there a revival in the making? Verwey said they are experiencing a few raindrops.

The Korean population is ten percent Christians, whereas Japan is less than one percent. So why is Korea the "Christian nation of the east" and not Japan? Verwey in his autobiography, attributes the success of Christianity in Korea to their penchant for prayer. "Korean Christians love God more than sleep, more than money, more than food or even the daily necessities of life. When they yield to Christ, they give Him their all."

My Japanese wife thinks Christianity is more successful in Korea because of their strong Confucianist culture. Koreans are famous for being more Confucianist than the Japanese. Showing respect up the hierarchy is extremely important, which means Jesus' Lordship in their lives is taken much more seriously.

Confucianism also demands loyalty, which is a facet of the feeling preference. In my book, *Where in the World Do I Belong??*, the Korean culture type is extroverted feeling. Christianity is a feeling type culture; therefore, it fits the Korean extroverted feeling culture. Koreans resonate with Christian feeling values such as love, loyalty, kindness, understanding, humility, harmony, compassion and empathy. Japan is an introverted sensing culture type, so may not resonate with Christianity as much as Korean culture does. Japanese are more focused on sensing aspects of religion (such as rituals and music) as opposed to the feeling aspects of it.

There is a saying in Japan that children are the hinge on the door that keeps the mother and father together. I asked Verwey about reaching Japanese in troubled or broken marriages and he said the problem is only going to get worse.

In 2007, a new law went into effect that gave Japanese wives the right to half their husbands estate upon divorce. This isn't anything new to us Americans, but in Japan its probably weakening the glue that has kept many marriages together. He said the government started classes to try to teach Japanese husbands how to say 'thank you' and 'I'm sorry'.

Boy, is Japan a country hurting for a spiritual revival or what?!

Japanese and victory in Christ.

One native Japanese Christian, who has been living in the US most of his life, told me that if you want to reach Japanese don't tell them to read Paul's epistles (Romans, Corinthians, etc). The epistles tell you what to do—which is okay for the American/European way of thinking but not for Japanese or Asians. He said Japanese won't listen

Japanese first want to see God's truth in other people's lives.

if you just tell them what to do. They might even go along with what you say but in their heart they don't believe it. The Japanese want to see the truth through other people's lives. When evangelizing Japanese you have to tell them to look at your life, and make their decision based on what they see. If they see the truth in your life and the lives of the people around you, they will probably make the decision to accept Christ as their Savior, too.

It seems to follow that missionaries in Japan and anyone sharing the gospel with the Japanese have to truly be walking in the Spirit themselves. They have to be experiencing victory in Christ for themselves. The problem is that Solomon, who has forty years experience in counseling Christians, estimates that "90 percent of all Christians never experience the abundant or victorious life" (*Handbook to Happiness*). In my experience and through my gift of discernment, I would agree with Solomon's estimate. Many people tell me it's not possible to judge whether someone is victorious or not; but one pastor pointed out all you have to do is look at the fruit. I agree, the proof is in the fruit, victorious lives produce spiritual fruit: love, joy, peace, patience, kindness, goodness, faithfulness, gentleness, and self-control. Spiritual fruit isn't produced through self-effort but through the walking in the Holy Spirit, which is the essence of a victorious life.

Living in the spirit versus sin conscience.

Different culture types (see my book *Where in the World Do I Belong??* for an explanation of culture types) filter and interpret God's truth in different ways. Each culture type has a unique view of the world and this also applies to their understanding of God. Pastors from different cultures illuminate the Word of God's truth in unexpected ways.

Joseph Prince is a pastor of a large church in Singapore. In a recent TV sermon he explained that the modern translation of the water of life flowing out of God's heart is not correct. The correct translation of the Hebrew/Greek word is not heart but stomach. Japanese proverbs describe someone who does evil as having a black stomach—instead of a black heart. They probably have a similar idea in the Chinese dominated culture of Singapore, and that is why he picked up on this translation difference.

Prince said that when we decide to do something—because we believe it is right or wrong—we are living under the law and the tree of knowledge of good and evil. We have to be living under the tree of life where our belly tells us if something is life or death. This is what he calls living in the spirit and not out of a sin conscience. If it feels like the life is dwindling within you then probably that thing or activity is death for you.

He said that the water of life flows not only from Gods belly but also from ours. For example, when we speak in tongues it flows from our belly and heals stomach and intestine problems, and female problems like cramps. He picked up a book at the bookstore and began reading it and realized it was on metaphysics. He put it down and later in the day had some diarrhea (IBS), and God told Him it was from holding that book. You touch death and it brings death in you, in your belly, where the waters of life flow.

9

Holy Spirit Revival

Jonathan Goforth, a missionary to China from 1888 to 1935, pointed out how the missionaries in Korea constantly prayed for a revival before it happened (starting in 1903). And after it happened in Korea, the missionaries in China also followed suit and began regular daily prayer for a revival in China. After visiting Korea, Goforth went from being a stationary missionary to traveling revivalist. He visited many churches and missionary stations in Manchuria (the part of China just above the Korean peninsula).

At his revival meetings, Goforth gave a sermon and then opened up for prayer from the congregation. He requested that no one say their regular prayers but instead what the Holy Spirit led them to pray for. "At the close of every address I, as far as possible, committed the control of the meeting to the guidance of the Holy Spirit." His revival meetings were like the day of Pentecost with the pouring out of the Holy Spirit upon churches packed with people.

On the day of Pentecost, Peter explained how we are filled with the Holy Spirit. Peter replied, "Repent and be baptized, every one of you, in the name of Jesus Christ for the forgiveness of your sins. And you will receive the gift of the Holy Spirit" (Acts 2:38). Those who accepted his message were baptized, and about three thousand were added to their number that day (Acts 2:41).

God did this same work, as the Pentecost, in Korea and China in 1908. Today, exactly one hundred years later, God still shows no favoritism and the very same outpouring of the Holy Spirit can happen here in Hawaii or even in Japan. But God showed Goforth that it's not possible until the very leaders in attendance of the church, small group, prayer meeting, etc, have removed the hindering things from their lives (e.g. personal sins, unresolved conflicts with others, unforgiveness, etc.). And sometimes that even meant a public confession of sins—which also led others to follow suit.

> *Church and ministry leaders can hinder the Holy Spirit if they have any unrepented sin in their lives.*

"We came to the final meeting. I had given my address, and the meeting was open for prayer. In the conduct of these meetings I experience, as a rule, no overburdening anxiety. I tell myself that if God does not choose to use this or that address to move His people, then He will probably use the one to follow. And if in some particular meeting no spiritual power becomes evident in the prayers then I close that meeting and wait upon God for an outpouring of His grace in the next one. This evening, however, there was a great burden upon me, and I found myself agonizing with God that He would remove the stone of hindrance, whatever it might be.

Dr. L- was leaning on the pulpit beside me. "Doctor!" I whispered, "I simply cannot account for the hindrance in your church. I've always had a conviction, in leading these meetings, that once all the foreign missionaries have removed any hindering things from their midst, then no power of the devil can prevent the Holy Spirit from being made manifest. Certainly, listening to you missionaries at your prayer meetings, I cannot imagine how there could be any hindrance on your part. Still, there is something holding us up."

I continued to pray, almost feverishly, that God would take the hindering stone away. Then suddenly a voice seemed to rebuke me. "Why all this anxiety? What are you fretting yourself about? Am I not sovereign? Can I not do My own work? Don't you know enough to 'stand still and see the salvation of the Lord?' " "Yes, Lord," I replied, "I'll do as you say. I'm tired out. I'll not even pray. I'll just 'stand still'" (BY MY SPIRIT By Jonathan Goforth).

The pastor of the church had previously humbled himself with his fellow pastor over a conflict but God was calling Him to make a public confession. "God's gifts were, therefore, withheld until a public confession from His servant had cleared the disgrace to His name." After the pastor of the church made a public confession of his sin, the rest of the leaders broke down and all the members of the church were on their knees repenting of their own sins. In these meetings long-time pastors, missionaries, leaders, elders, church members, and even non-Christian newcomers were convicted, repented, and baptized by the Holy Spirit. During these meetings heartfelt, fervent prayer and tears were constantly flowing. The floors of the churches were wet with the tears of relief from the mercy of God.

Just as it was two thousand years ago at Pentecost, and a hundred years ago in Korea and China, this level of revival is available to us on the individual, church, and national (cultural) level—if only we would open our lives to each other and the Holy Spirit.

Christians open their lives to the Holy Spirit and each other.

One person from Singapore commented on my blog about Holy Spirit Revival: "Care to confess YOUR personal sins in public?"

I have confessed some of my personal sins in my writing in hopes that it would help others, for example, in my partial testimony and my personal struggles brought to light through God speaking to my dreams.

Years ago, when I attended A.A., I learned that 'our secrets kept us sick'. This was a belief I lived by for many years and throughout my years of receiving personal counseling. I turned it into an inner vow that I had to break and allow the Holy Spirit to guide me instead. We are not called to public humiliation and destroying our reputation, but we must get rid of anything that hinders the Holy Spirit. Goforth continually told church leadership if they have something to hide (unrepented sin) it would hinder the Holy Spirit in their lives and the members of their church. As they felt convicted by the Holy Spirit, they were moved to confess to the congregation the nature of their sin (adultery, theft, unresolved conflict, unforgiveness, jealousy, etc, etc.). Of course, our leaders are no more perfect than us, but we have to remember as leaders they can hinder the Holy Spirit in a group.

Some people might have a difficulty opening up to others because they have never done it or because they want to protect themselves. One Christian said he doesn't want to be too transparent because that might cause others to fall. I assume he means that others will gossip about him or use the information against him. As Christians, God, through His Word, has commanded us to "confess your sins to each other and pray for each other so that you may be healed" and through this we are victorious over our sins. Our church recommends using the MiniChurch (a small prayer and Bible study group) or accountability partners as the place for this. We don't need to confess sins that God has already forgiven us for, just what the Holy Spirit puts on our heart. Repenting of our sins to our brothers and sisters also keeps us accountable so we don't go back to our sin.

Confess your sins to each other and hold each other accountable.

Christian Revival in the US, Asia and the Middle East.

My mother, a retired historian, pointed out how there is so much Christian history we never hear about. For example, a 1700s Christian revival in the US was the impetus for the independence movement (against England). There are also current events, like Christian revivals spreading across other regions of the world, that we don't hear about. Few Christians realized the intense power of the Holy Spirit manifest in other countries. One missionary leader said, in his experience, in the countries that persecute Christians the Holy Spirit is felt stronger. God promises to not give us more than we can handle, therefore, during persecution His Spirit's grace and power works through us even more strongly to make the impossible possible. Another Christian pointed out that the Holy Spirit is stronger where it hasn't been before. In the 1800's Christianity was introduced to Hawaiians for the first time. Hawaii's Great Awakening "broke out on the Island of Hawaii in 1837 and spread throughout the kingdom. By the 1850s the census showed that 96% of Hawaiians were Christians!" (Christian Voice of Hawaii)

In 2008, I attended a sister church in Japan and it was the strongest I have ever felt the Holy Spirit in a church service. Throughout the bilingual worship and bilingual sermon I was continuously teary-eyed from the immense feeling of the mercy and relief of the Holy Spirit present in that church. Half the songs I didn't understand because they were in Japanese and the sermon was as good as any here in Hawaii, but the Spirit manifestation was unlike any I have experienced. In Japan, Christians are not politically or physically persecuted but they are socially outcast. There is strong pressure to conform to socially accepted ways in Japan. Christians are reported to be only one or two percent of the Japanese population so they are not only a highly marginalized group but clearly socially ostracized. The pastor mentioned it's a well known fact that it's hard to keep your faith in Japan.

In Japan, the manifestation of the Holy Spirit was unlike any I have experienced.

Christianity Today reports the Chinese government is easing restrictions and the house-church movement is coming out of secrecy and proclaiming their faith through public gatherings. One Associated Content reporter said, "Chinese house churches, in the country which greatly persecute Christians, plan to send 100,000 through many Muslim nations and back to Israel." Chinese are so moved by their faith and the Spirit that they are willing to pass through dangerous Muslim, Middle Eastern countries and witness to them in the process.

One author documents in his blog the massive increase in Muslim conversions to Christianity in Middle Eastern countries like Afghanistan, Iraq, Iran, Egypt, Sudan, Uzbekistan, and Kazakhstan. The manifestation of the Holy Spirit has even taken the form of dreams and visions. He said, "One of the most dramatic developments is that many Muslims throughout the Middle East and even in the United States are seeing dreams and visions of Jesus. They are coming into churches explaining that they have already converted and now need a Bible and guidance on how to follow Jesus. This is in fulfillment of Biblical prophecy. The Hebrew Prophet Joel told us that 'in the last days, I will pour out my Spirit on all people. Your sons and daughters will prophesy, your old men will dream dreams, your young men will see visions. Even on my servants, both men and women, I will pour out my Spirit in those days....And everyone who calls on the name of the LORD will be saved' (Joel 2:28-32)."

Acknowledgments

I would like to say a big thank you to Rheba Massey for her guidance. I would also like to thank the pastors and members of Hope Chapel West Oahu for their contributions to my growth as a Christian. Above all, sincere praise and gratitude to the Lord Jesus Christ for bringing me this far, and His inspiration and insight in my writing. He's Alive!

About the Author

Brent Massey is an Christian author, publisher, teacher, and MBTI Qualified Practitioner. He lives in Hawaii and is also the author of *Culture Shock! Hawaii* and *Where in the World Do I Belong??*.

He can be contacted at brentmassey@yahoo.com or brentmassey@brentmassey.com. He is interested in hearing from people from around the world.

www.ingramcontent.com/pod-product-compliance
Lightning Source LLC
Chambersburg PA
CBHW022114280326
41953CB00007B/391